'Be my witnesses'

'Kieran has a passion for the lost that shows. Better still that passion is directed not by the wisdom of men, but by the Word of God. You will find here both encouragement to be witnesses, and direction on how in doing that, to be faithful to Scripture, to the lost, and most of all, to the Lord, our Saviour.'

Dr R. C. Sproul Jr
Teaching Fellow at Ligonier Ministries; Founder of Highlands Ministries

'I have long been convinced that the church is rapidly losing touch with the world and that many Christians have lost the ability to interact effectively with unbelievers. This book is an urgently needed wake-up call! Biblical, sensible and immensely practical, it could transform the way its readers go about "gossiping the gospel". I dare you to read it!'

John Blanchard
International conference speaker and author

'This is a perfectly splendid book on being a witness to Jesus Christ. It is splendid for the following reasons: it is succinct and readable; it develops the dynamic logic of bearing testimony to Jesus Christ and draws us into the narrative; it does not take the Christian reader on a guilt trip; it is rather an encouragement to experience the enabling grace of the Lord who makes his disciples fishers of men — as the Master once affirmed — so that we find a kindling response ... "I can do this; I must do this." Although the author recognizes that our life and good works are indispensable he does not absolutize those marks of new life in Christ as completely satisfying the Lord's command that we should be his witnesses. He gently persuades us to affirm with our own words whose we are and whom we serve. There can scarcely be a more relevant book for the youngest or most mature Christian to read than this.'

Geoff Thomas
Author, conference speaker and pastor

'In this easy to read book Kieran Beville expresses his passionate concern for Christians to be witnesses to the gospel. He helpfully draws out principles from a range of New Testament passages and applies them in very practical ways to our daily lives. On a number of occasions in the book Kieran moves naturally from encouraging gospel witness to proclaiming the gospel itself! He reminds us that our witness is not only what we say but what we are, and affirms the priority of living a consistent Christian life every day.'

Peter Milsom
Director of Affinity; and former director of UFM Worldwide

'I am impressed with the full-orbed and thoughtful presentation regarding evangelism and missions found in this well-written work by Kieran Beville. Readers will be encouraged not only to think clearly about the truthfulness of the gospel message, but will be guided toward a new zeal for practical and faithful application in life and ministry. It is a joy to recommend this fine work.'

David S. Dockery
President, Union University, Jackson, Tennessee, USA

'Be my witnesses'

Christ's last words:
our first concern

Kieran Beville

 BOOKS

EP BOOKS
Faverdale North
Darlington
DL3 0PH, England

www.epbooks.org
sales@epbooks.org

EP BOOKS are distributed in the USA by:
JPL Fulfillment
3741 Linden Avenue Southeast,
Grand Rapids, MI 49548.

E-mail: sales@jplfulfillment.com
Tel: 877.683.6935

First published 2013

British Library Cataloguing in Publication Data available
ISBN: 978-0-85234-926-7

Contents

	Page
Foreword	7
1. Christ's last words: our first concern	9
2. Dispelling the myth	27
3. Defining a Christian	43
4. Befriending sinners	53
5. Relational evangelism	65
6. Let's go fishing!	83
7. Developing a theology of evangelism	107
8. Practical advice	131
Conclusion	157

Foreword

The task of being witnesses confronts believers every day of their lives. They are constantly faced with the challenge of seizing opportunities to speak spiritual truths, of explaining these truths accurately, and of leading the listener appropriately for a response. With these challenges, many questions are raised and fears aroused.

Kieran Beville's book offers guidance to every sincere Christian in the duty of sharing the gospel. It fills many gaps and misunderstandings, frees believers from being bound to one method of evangelism, upholds relational evangelism and offers many practical guidelines for being faithful witnesses.

The book never departs from the necessity of the heart of the witness being in dynamic relationship with Christ. To do so, the witness must be totally grounded and empowered by the truth of the gospel. He or she also seeks to share this gospel with the lost that they may have the chance to partake of it also. Thus the gospel is the power of God to believer and non-believer.

Following the example of Christ, a believer never disassociates from nonbelievers. In constant acts of love, the Christian witness innovates in communicating the hope within. This is best achieved in building genuine relationships, a method often de-emphasized. But in all attempts, believers are to trust the Lord for the outcome. The witness can reach an unbeliever's ears, but it is only the Holy Spirit that reaches the heart.

With countless books on evangelism, this book fills in many of the fractures in effective witnessing, offers gems of experienced advice, helps protect from many pitfalls, responds to important unanswered questions, and keeps the gospel at the centre.

I enjoyed reading this work at a time when I noted in my regular devotions in Isaiah the repeated reminder of the Lord to his people that they were his witnesses (e.g. Isaiah 43:10, 12; 44:8). It is our honour to serve the Lord as fellow witnesses.

Dr Imad N. Shehadeh
President and Senior Professor of Theology
Jordan Evangelical Theological Seminary
Pastor, Rabia Baptist Church, Amman, Jordan

1

Christ's last words:
our first concern

*'But you will receive power when the Holy Spirit has come
upon you, and you will be my witnesses in Jerusalem and in
all Judea and Samaria, and to the end of the earth'*

(Acts 1:8).

The Christian has a sacred duty to seek the lost and to do so diligently by sharing with them the good news of the gospel of Christ so that they can join in vibrant God-centred worship, thereby giving glory to God as Creator and Redeemer. Though not every believer is a God-gifted evangelist all believers are called to be witnesses. Jesus said, 'But you will receive power when the Holy Spirit has come upon you, and you will be my witnesses in Jerusalem and in all Judea and Samaria, and to the end of the earth' (Acts 1:8). They were the last words Christ spoke on earth, his parting words to his disciples. His last words should be our first concern. These words have a very special significance. The last words spoken by a person on earth have great importance. We tend to think often about the last words of loved ones. Such words constitute a kind of last will and testament. If we love the person who spoke those words then we try to ensure that their last expressed wish is carried out. Love motivates us to do this.

These were prophetic words from Christ to these particular disciples but they are also words which relate to us. Witnessing for Christ is not only about speaking words it is also about 'being'. In other words, it is about what we are and how we live as well as what we say. We have a message to communicate but we also have a Master to emulate.

What is a witness?

Sometimes people are called to court to bear witness to the truth. They are key people in the proceedings because they have vital first-hand information. They have seen something or heard something that needs to be brought to light. The apostle John said, 'That which was from the beginning, which we have heard, which we have seen with our eyes, which we have looked at and our hands have touched — this we proclaim concerning the Word of life' (1 John 1:1, NIV). As witnesses of Christ it is crucial for us to have that first-hand experience of Jesus. We must have that living, dynamic relationship with Jesus if we are going to be effective witnesses. So being effective witnesses depends on the quality of our relationship with Christ. It is not about religion, rather it is about relationship. The apostle Peter said, 'For we did not follow cleverly devised myths when we made known to you the power and coming of our Lord Jesus Christ, but we were eyewitnesses of his majesty' (2 Peter 1:16).

All believers are potential witnesses inasmuch as we have first-hand experience of God's redeeming love. But we need to have the courage and confidence to actively engage in communicating that to others. It is the power of God that enables us to be transformed from weaklings to witnesses. What are we witnesses to? We are to be witnesses to the truth. In other words, we are to bear witness to the unique and universal claims of Christ, that he is the way, the truth and the life and that there is no other name by which people can be saved (John 14:6; Acts 4:12-13). In order to do this effectively believers have a duty to familiarize themselves with the basics of the gospel message so they can share their faith accurately and articulately with those with whom the Lord brings them into contact. The leadership of every church has a responsibility to equip its members to do this. This process will commence with prayer and it will continue in prayer. We must recognize that prayer is a crucial element in any successful efforts to evangelize the lost.

The apostle Paul, who may have been the greatest evangelist who ever lived (except for Jesus), once asked the Ephesian Christians to pray for him, 'that words may be given to me in opening my mouth boldly to proclaim the mystery of the gospel ... that I may declare it boldly, as I ought to speak' (Ephesians 6:19-20). He also asked the Colossian Christians to pray for him, 'that God may open to us a door for the word, to declare the mystery of Christ ... that I may make it clear, which is how I ought to speak' (Colossians 4:3-4).

One of the first things Jesus' disciples did, after he told them they would be his witnesses, was to pray (Acts 1:14). Many Christians are afraid of 'evangelism' but everybody can pray, and that is part of the process of witnessing.

We have a biblical mandate for evangelism. Jesus said, 'Go therefore and make disciples of all nations, baptizing them in the name of the Father and of the Son and of the Holy Spirit, teaching them to observe all that I have commanded you. And behold, I am with you always, to the end of the age' (Matthew 28:19-20). Our authority for this commission comes from Jesus and has the force of a command. Jesus said, 'Whoever has my commandments and keeps them, he it is who loves me' (John 14:21). One way to demonstrate our love for Christ is to obey this command.

A witness is someone who sees or experiences something and tells others about it. Witnesses have first-hand knowledge to which they can bear testimony. A witness tells of what he saw, heard and experienced. A witness for Jesus Christ is simply someone who tells others what they know about him. That means telling others who Jesus is and what he came to earth to do. This means telling others that Jesus is the way of salvation.

Clearly you and I have never seen Jesus with our own eyes or heard him teach with our physical ears. We were not eyewitnesses to his miracles, his death on the cross, or his resurrection from the grave. But every true Christian has direct knowledge and experience of Jesus. The believer has first-hand experience regarding the fact that the gospel, 'is the power of God for salvation to everyone who believes' (Romans 1:16). We can testify to the fact that, 'if you confess with your mouth that Jesus is Lord and believe in your heart that God raised him from the dead, you will be saved' (Romans 10:9). We can do this because this is our personal experience. We bear testimony to the reality that, 'if anyone is in Christ, he is a new creation. The old has passed away; behold, the new has come' (2 Corinthians 5:17). We know what it is to have our sins forgiven (Romans 4:7-8) and to have peace with God (Romans 5:1). We know what it means to be free from eternal condemnation (Romans 8:1), to no longer have the wrath of God hanging over our heads (John 3:36). We can bear testimony to the reality that our sins have been cast into the depths of the sea (Micah 7:19). We can say

12

with confidence that our sins are removed from us as far as the east is from the west (Psalm 103:12). We are witnesses to the fact that God's mercy to us in Jesus Christ is far greater than the sum total of all our sins (1 Timothy 1:15-16). God has put our sins out of sight, out of mind, out of reach and out of existence through Christ the atoning sacrifice for our sins. We can invite others to enter this happy, guilt-free, condemnation-free condition if they will repent and put their trust in Jesus and his completed work at Calvary.

So, having known and experienced these things, we are to bear witness to them, especially to the one who brought them to pass in our lives: Jesus, who is the Christ, the Son of God, and the only Saviour of sinners (John 20:31; 1 John 5:11-12).

The power to be effective witnesses comes from God. It does not come from our own strength. Success is not determined by any natural abilities we may have, or by how clever we are, or from resolving to work as hard as we can. Hence, our effectiveness does not depend on finding some secret formula for witnessing. There is no special methodology. There is no such thing as the right evangelism programme. Paul acknowledged that we are not adequate in ourselves for such a task: 'Not that we are sufficient in ourselves to claim anything as coming from us, but our sufficiency is from God, who has made us competent' (2 Corinthians 3:5-6). The fact that we are utterly dependent on the Holy Spirit to be effective witnesses is both humbling and encouraging because it means any success we achieve ultimately depends on him, not us.

The best method for sharing our faith is simply to bear faithful, consistent testimony in word and deed to the reality of God in our lives. Bearing witness is an intentional process of communicating the truth which is a natural outcome of communion with God. As Jesus said, 'I am the vine; you are the branches. Whoever abides in me and I in him, he it is that bears much fruit, for apart from me you can do nothing' (John 15:5).

We must remember that any evangelistic success we have is due solely to the power of the Holy Spirit working in us and through us. It is the Holy Spirit who opens the eyes, minds and hearts of unbelievers to be receptive and responsive to the gospel.

Some have used this as an excuse not to witness or get involved in the work of evangelism, taking the attitude that since God is sovereign he will make sure his elect are saved regardless of whether we witness or not. But to do this ignores the fact we are commanded to spread the gospel. God uses various means to accomplish his sovereign purposes, and believers are instrumental in achieving God's purposes. Thus we have the presence and power of the Holy Spirit to enable us to be Christ's witnesses.

Jesus said, '...you will be my witnesses in Jerusalem and in all Judea and Samaria, and to the end of the earth' (Acts 1:8). Here is an image of concentric circles. At the centre is our 'Jerusalem', that is, whatever location we inhabit. It consists of the people we work with, the people who live next door, the people we do business with and the people we see on a regular basis as we go about our daily lives. For us, 'Judea' extends a little further afield in the region where we live, and 'Samaria' further extends the circumference of our sphere of influence to more remote places, perhaps in our own land. The 'ends of the earth' are the remotest places from our immediate experience. This will vary, depending on where we live but it certainly evokes an image of cross-cultural communication. There is a local, regional, national and international dimension to the dissemination of the gospel. It is parochial and global.

The point is that those converted to Christ are commissioned and charged with the task of reaching people with the gospel. We have a mission to fulfil. The methods we use to witness will vary according to the culture, the situation and the people we encounter. But one thing never changes — namely, that we have a mandate from our Saviour to be his witnesses wherever we are. May the Lord graciously enable us through the power of the Holy Spirit to be faithful and fervent witnesses for Jesus!

On one occasion Peter and John were ordered not to speak or teach in the name of Jesus any longer, to which they replied, 'we cannot but speak of what we have seen and heard' (Acts 4:20). Such was their experience of Jesus that they could not stop talking about him. How much of this fervour is evident in the saints today?

The cost of confessing Christ

The Greek word Jesus used for 'witnesses' in Acts 1:8 eventually came to mean 'martyr'. In fact, it is basically the same word used in Revelation where John says, 'I saw under the altar the souls of those who had been slain for the word of God and for the witness they had borne' (Revelation 6:9). Being witnesses for Christ has cost many Christians their lives historically, and even today in certain parts of the world it can cost you your freedom or even your life.

In the New Testament, John the Baptist was beheaded (Matthew 14:10), Stephen was stoned to death (Acts 7:54-60) and the apostle James was put to death by the sword (Acts 12:1-2). Other unnamed Christians also sealed their witness for Christ with their life's blood. Before Paul was converted he used to persecute Christians unmercifully. He said, 'I not only locked up many of the saints in prison after receiving authority from the chief priests, but when they were put to death I cast my vote against them' (Acts 26:10).

Christians lost their lives during an outbreak of persecution under the Roman emperor Nero (AD 54 – AD 68). This continued under the emperor Domitian (AD 81 – AD 96). Hence, through the apostle John, Christ encouraged his disciples living in Smyrna to, 'Be faithful unto death' (Revelation 2:10). He also assured his followers living in Pergamum that he was pleased with them for not denying the faith even at great personal cost, 'Yet you hold fast my name, and you did not deny my faith even in the days of Antipas my faithful witness, who was killed among you, where Satan dwells' (Revelation 2:13).

Many today remain faithful witnesses in places where Satan dwells. Many have been willing to bear testimony to Jesus even when imprisoned and tortured. Many have been faithful unto death. They are a challenge to us. In the Western world we might face ridicule and rejection. We might face mockery and verbal hostility but we have freedom from persecution that our fellow believers in many other parts of the world do not enjoy.

In 1956, Jim Elliot and four other missionaries landed their aeroplane on a remote beach in Eastern Ecuador. Two days later they were speared and hacked to death by warriors from the Auca Indian tribe with whom they had hoped to share the gospel.

We get reports from clandestine missionaries in places like North Korea, Sudan, Pakistan and various Muslim countries about brothers and sisters in Christ who are being tortured and killed simply because they are Christians, or because they have refused to deny their Saviour. This must challenge the complacency of those who take their freedom for granted.

Christ's last words: our first concern

Not every Christian is called upon to seal their witness as a martyr. But every Christian is called to be a witness for Christ irrespective of the cost. There will always be a cost to following Christ and being faithful witnesses for the Lord. Jesus spoke of the cost of being a disciple: 'For which of you, desiring to build a tower, does not first sit down and count the cost, whether he has enough to complete it?' (Luke 14:28). Before we begin any serious project it is wise to count the cost. The call to follow Christ is a serious undertaking. Many ignore the call. Others contemplate it but decline to follow Jesus. Some follow for a time but are unwilling to go all the way. Counting the cost of discipleship involves forsaking sin. It involves the surrender of our will to the will of God. What will it cost the self to put Christ first in all things? Following Jesus means forsaking the world. But when we are fully satisfied with the Lord we do not need what the world has to offer. The Christian has to resist the allurement of the world and stand firm against worldly opposition, for the world is opposed to the things of God. The Christian will face temptations. Lust, pride, envy, covetousness and greed distort our thinking and might even offer the illusion of a better life in the world. The cost of following Christ will involve self-denial.

But consider the cost of not being a Christian. If a person invests his/her soul in the world they will be spiritually bankrupt. Ultimately there is great gain in following Christ. But there will be great loss for those who do not follow him. They will lose the forgiving love of God. They will lose the redeeming power of Christ. They will lose the comforting presence of the Holy Spirit. They will lose the assuring promises of his holy Word. They will miss out on the joy of serving the Lord and the blessed hope of eternity in his glorious presence. There is infinitely more to gain than can be lost because we swap our rags for robes of righteousness.

Jesus asked the rhetorical question, 'For what will it profit a man if he gains the whole world and forfeits his soul?' (Matthew 16:26). It is clear that potential disciples are warned to count the cost and be prepared to pay the price no matter what. In order to do this we will need the enabling grace of the Holy Spirit.

Nobody wants to be a martyr. We admire people who have the courage to face hardship and persecution for the sake of Christ, but we don't want to be one of them. The thought that bearing witness for Christ might actually cost something is one we do not relish. Most of us will never have to shed our life's blood for the sake of the gospel but there will be unpleasant moments of ridicule and/or rejection. Jesus said, 'Blessed are you when others revile you and persecute you and utter all kinds of evil against you falsely on my account' (Matthew 5:11). We might well be insulted and persecuted for the sake of Christ, even if that persecution means only being scoffed at. But if we are honest with ourselves we will have to admit that this is one 'blessing' we would rather do without.

Luke records in Acts that the apostles were arrested, imprisoned, flogged and warned not to speak in the name of Jesus any more. But undaunted, 'they left ... rejoicing that they were counted worthy to suffer dishonour for the name' (Acts 5:40-41). How many of us would react like they did in the face of such opposition, hostility and persecution? This is evidence of the enabling power of the Holy Spirit. We cannot endure such things in our own strength. It is when our courage fails that the Holy Spirit supplies power. Even the thick-skinned and those who relish a good fight will be found wanting in their own strength. To be effective witnesses we need the empowering of the Holy Spirit.

Evangelism and witnessing

What is the relationship between evangelism and witnessing? Do the words 'evangelism' and 'witnessing' always refer to the same thing? We tend to use them as if their meanings were identical. But in Scripture they are not interchangeable. Though there is some obvious overlap, being a witness for Christ does not always involve evangelism in the strict sense of presenting the gospel message. Sharing the gospel message is one way of witnessing for Christ. Of course there should be times when our witness for Christ involves evangelism: that is an intentional and active process of communicating the message of the gospel.

In the New Testament one of the primary Greek words for 'preach' (*euaggelizo*), along with the word for 'gospel' (*euaggelion*) and the word for 'evangelist' (*euaggelistes*) are all basically the same. For example, the primary Greek word for 'preach' (*euaggelizo*) means 'to announce good news' or to 'preach the gospel'.

Luke records the angel saying to the shepherds, 'Fear not, for behold, I bring you good news of great joy that will be for all the people. For unto you is born this day in the city of David a Saviour, who is Christ the Lord' (Luke 2:10-11). Jesus said, 'The Spirit of the Lord is upon me, because he has anointed me to proclaim good news' (Luke 4:18). In Acts, we are told that those who fled Jerusalem because of persecution, 'went about preaching the word' (Acts 8:4). In Scripture, then, one of the primary Greek words for 'preaching' refers specifically to preaching the gospel of salvation. Scripture asks: 'But how are they to call on him in whom they have not believed? And how are they to believe in him of whom they have never heard? And how are they to hear without someone preaching [*kerusso*]?' (Romans 10:14).

The Greek word translated 'gospel' (*euaggelion*) literally means 'good news'. Hence, Mark opens his account of the Lord's life by calling it, 'The beginning of the gospel of Jesus Christ, the Son of God' (Mark 1:1). It is recorded that Peter said, 'Brothers, you know that in the early days God made a choice among you, that by my mouth the Gentiles should hear the word of the gospel and believe' (Acts 15:7). And Paul declared, 'Now I would remind you, brothers, of the gospel I preached to you, which you received, in which you stand, and by which you are being saved, if you hold fast to the word I preached to you' (1 Corinthians 15:1-2). There can be no confusion as to what this gospel is because he goes on to summarize it by saying that, 'Christ died for our sins in accordance with the Scriptures, that he was buried, that he was raised on the third day in accordance with the Scriptures' (Corinthians 15:3-4). So, 'gospel' refers to a specific message, namely the message of salvation from the penalty and guilt of sin through the atoning sacrifice of Christ.

The Greek word translated 'evangelist' (*euaggelistes*) means 'a bringer of good news'. Thus it refers to a person who preaches, teaches, and/or explains the good news of the gospel. Paul, writing to the Ephesians, says that God, 'gave the apostles, the prophets, the evangelists, the pastors and teachers, to equip the saints for the work of ministry, for building up the body of Christ' (Ephesians 4:11-12). This suggests the Holy Spirit has given some individuals in the Church a special gift for telling others how they can be saved. Certainly the evangelist has a role in training (equipping) Christians to share their faith with non-Christians by, 'being prepared to make a defence to anyone who asks you for a reason for the hope that is in you' (1 Peter 3:15). Paul instructed Timothy (a pastor) to 'do the work of an evangelist' (2 Timothy 4:5). This suggests that pastors should engage in evangelism, either by preaching evangelistically or by some other means. But essentially an evangelist is someone who has a specific gift to bring a special message (the gospel) to unsaved sinners.

Thus evangelism is a work which focusses on telling others about who Jesus is and why he came into the world. The message of the evangelist is that every person needs to be saved. The evangelist tells people how they can be saved. Obviously, evangelism involves witnessing (in word) but witnessing does not necessarily involve evangelism, at least not in the sense of speaking directly about God's plan for saving sinners through Jesus Christ.

Apart from the spoken witness there can also be a silent witness. When someone notices that you do not use coarse language or take the Lord's name in vain and they find out it is because you are a Christian, you are bearing a witness concerning Jesus Christ. When you, like the Old Testament character Joseph, refuse to give in to the adulterous advances of a co-worker or boss (as Joseph resisted the advances of his master's wife, Genesis 39:7-12) you are bearing testimony through purity of life. When you, like Moses, are found 'choosing rather to be mistreated with the people of God than to enjoy the fleeting pleasures of sin' (Hebrews 11:25), you are witnessing for God. When you, like Daniel, Peter and the apostles, choose to obey God rather than men (Daniel 6:10; Acts 5:27-29) you are witnessing. When you, like Job, or Shadrach, Meshach and Abednego, testify by word and deed that you are going to trust the Lord and hope in him even if he doesn't rescue you from your plight (Job 13:15; Daniel 3:17-18), you are faithfully witnessing. When your neighbours, work colleagues, fellow students and acquaintances come and ask you for prayer for themselves or for others that they care about they do so because they have observed your faithful witness.

Witnessing does not have to include a presentation of the gospel message. Hopefully our testimony will lead to such opportunities but as long as we are being faithful to Christ and his Word in whatever situation we find ourselves, we are fulfilling the mandate to be his witnesses (Acts 1:8). We must do so regardless of whether we get a chance to explain God's plan of salvation or not. Now the other side of the coin is that we are to follow the instruction of Peter by, 'always being prepared to make a defence to anyone who asks you for a reason for the hope that is in you' (1 Peter 3:15). In other words, we should always be ready to evangelize by sharing our faith and being ready to explain the plan of salvation to anyone who asks us or gives us the opportunity.

Paul and Silas witnessed to their faith in Christ by praying and singing hymns of praise to God in the middle of the night, even though they were in jail with their feet in stocks. Their testimony helped opened the door for them to share the gospel with their jailer when an earthquake drove him to ask, 'Sirs, what must I do to be saved?' (Acts 16:30). This witness led to the opportunity to answer a question concerning the way of salvation. So it ought to be with us; our witness should lead to opportunities to speak about the way of salvation. We must bear testimony through faithful living and be prepared to answer the questions when they come. This does not mean that we have to be passive respondents to the initiative of others. We can and should be proactive in seeking out opportunities to enter conversations about spiritual matters so that we can share the message of the gospel.

Paul wrote to the Colossians: '...pray ... that God may open to us a door for the word, to declare the mystery of Christ ... that I may make it clear, which is how I ought to speak. Walk in wisdom toward outsiders, making the best use of the time. Let your speech always be gracious, seasoned with salt, so that you may know how you ought to answer each person' (Colossians 4:2-6). The Christian is to be a faithful witness to Christ's gracious power at work in his life whether he is at home, at work, at school, away on a business trip or on vacation.

An intentional process

Many Christians are fearful of evangelism. They feel it is not their gift. They feel such work should be left to the evangelism team. Ideally the Christian should be intentional about evangelism, seeking out opportunities to speak about Jesus. However, if the thought of evangelism makes your knees tremble then just focus on being a faithful witness and evangelism will happen in a natural way in the course of conversations about what makes you tick. Remember the Holy Spirit can embolden and enlighten us so that we have the courage and clarity for the moment.

There are a number of things the Christian should do in this intentional process in order to be effective witnesses. Just as we were saved 'by grace through faith' (Ephesians 2:8-9), so we must learn to live each day in humble reliance upon God's grace (Galatians 3:2-3). This means depending on the Lord to enable us to do what he expects, which involves bearing witness.

In Colossians 4 Paul asks his fellow believers to pray that he might have opportunity to proclaim the gospel. If we want to be effective in evangelism we should begin by praying for opportunities. If Paul felt he needed the prayers of the saints to sustain him in his evangelistic efforts, how much more do we need to pray for each other and for ourselves when it comes to being witnesses for Christ? If we are really serious about being witnesses then we need to make it a matter of fervent and frequent prayer. We need to ask the Lord to open up doors for us to share the gospel with those who need to hear it and to be specific about this.

But it does not stop there. If we truly desire to share our faith with the lost we must look for opportunities. Having prayed God would open doors for us to share the gospel with others, we must then keep our eyes open for those openings that he sends our way in answer to our prayers. The apostle John once wrote about the confidence Christians can have that God will answer prayer, 'And this is the confidence that we have toward him, that if we ask anything according to his will he hears us. And if we know that he hears us in whatever we ask, we know that we have the requests that we have asked of him' (1 John 5:14-15). Whenever our prayers are in harmony with God's will we can be sure they will be answered. Can we be any more certain we are praying according to God's sovereign will than when we ask for opportunities to carry out the mandate of the Great Commission? We know the Lord's desire is for us to bear witness (Acts 1:8) and if we share this desire (and that is reflected in our prayers) we may be confident that the Lord will bless us with opportunities to speak of his saving power.

I once heard the story of a church in a land that was experiencing drought. The pastor suggested that the congregation meet at the farm of one of its members, to pray for rain. The people gathered and as the pastor stood to pray he noticed a little girl was the only one who had brought an umbrella! James said that when we pray we should, 'ask in faith, with no doubting' (James 1:6). If we are praying for opportunities to share the gospel we should also be on the lookout for those opportunities. This raises the questions: are we praying earnestly, and are we watching expectantly for doors to open?

But if we are to make full use of such opportunities we must be equipped to share the gospel with others. That means preparing ourselves so we know what to do and what to say when the Lord opens those doors of opportunity for which we have prayed. This is how we make 'the best use of the time' (Colossians 4:5). Both Paul and Peter agree about the manner in which we are to communicate the gospel message to others. Paul says, 'Let your speech always be gracious, seasoned with salt, so that you may know how you ought to answer each person' (Colossians 4:6). Peter instructs that such communication should be conducted with gentleness and respect (1 Peter 3:16).

Peter preached fearlessly in the power of the Holy Spirit on the Day of Pentecost explaining that the Jews had crucified the Messiah and the people were pierced to the heart. They were under the convicting power of the Holy Spirit — so much so that they asked, '...what shall we do?' (Acts 2:37) and Peter guided them to repent and believe. Philip encountered a man from Ethiopia, who asked questions about what he had been reading from Isaiah. It is recorded in Acts that, 'Philip opened his mouth, and beginning with this Scripture he told him the good news about Jesus' (Acts 8:35). The outcome, in this instance, was that the man confessed faith in Christ and was saved. Philip was able to explain the Scriptures to him. So we need to ask ourselves, if we encountered such an opportunity would we be able to explain the Scriptures? Are we in such a state of preparedness to take advantage of the opportunities that come our way? The jailer at Philippi asked Paul and Silas, '...what must I do to be saved?' (Acts 16:30). He was converted. Would you be able to lead him to salvation?

Suppose a friend or acquaintance has been recently diagnosed with a serious, life-threatening illness and he confided in you that he is afraid of dying. Would you be able to take him through the basics of the gospel? Suppose a co-worker takes notice of your gentle and friendly demeanour at work, or the fact you don't use foul language, or take the Lord's name in vain, or the fact you do your work without complaining or cutting corners and out of curiosity she asks you, 'Why?' Would you be able to give an account and answer by explaining the way of salvation? Sadly, some Christians would not. And yet this is precisely what Paul and Peter, in their respective passages, said we should be ready to do.

Obviously we need the enabling grace of God to be effective witnesses. But depending on his grace does not mean we should passively wait to be infused with wisdom. Depending on God's grace includes making use of the means of grace he has already provided for us. Thus we should immerse ourselves in Scripture so that we are able to tell others what God's Word says. Paul told Timothy that, 'All Scripture is breathed out by God and profitable for teaching, for reproof, for correction, and for training in righteousness, that the man of God may be competent, equipped for every good work' (2 Timothy 3:16-17). This work includes the work of evangelism. We should submit ourselves to training by gifted evangelists. We need to pray, watch and prepare for opportunities to tell others the way of salvation.

2
Dispelling the myth

'And in Antioch the disciples were first called Christians'
(Acts 11:26).

Recently I read a story about a man who killed his pet parrot because it kept calling him names. The man had spent months trying to teach the bird to say 'hello' and 'goodbye' but the creature seemed uninterested in learning this vocabulary. Finally, in a fit of rage the man called his bird an 'idiot', along with several other unflattering names, whereupon the parrot began repeating the insults every time his owner passed by. So in another fit of anger the man killed the bird.

A nickname

None of us like to be called derogatory names. We do not like having disparaging labels attached to us, in part because they wound our pride, demean our character, and call our integrity into question. One of the cruellest things children do is call each other names. Name-calling does not end in childhood. Adults often place labels on people they dislike.

First-century Christians were identified as people who belonged to Christ. The early Christians were people who openly identified themselves with Christ. The name 'Christian' was neither a neutral nor complimentary designation. Rather, it was a term of derision. In other words it was a contemptuous nickname bestowed on the followers of Jesus by those who did not like them. That is why the apostle Peter said, '... if anyone suffers as a Christian, let him not be ashamed, but let him glorify God in that name' (1 Peter 4:15-16).

In many countries there are few negative repercussions involved in identifying with Christ. But there are still places today where the name 'Christian' is spoken with contempt, derision, or outright hatred. For Christians living in Muslim countries there is more to fear than name-calling. Their lives are often in danger. In places where persecution is a very real possibility, people do not call themselves 'Christians' lightly. Indeed, persecution will weed out those who pretend to be Christians as well as those who have a shallow faith.

What is a Christian? Let us take the advice of Paul: 'Examine yourselves, to see whether you are in the faith' (2 Corinthians 13:5). Many churches have people sitting in their services Sunday after Sunday who think they know what a Christian is, but don't. Thus we need to set aside preconceived notions and find the biblical answer to the question, 'What is a Christian?' If we are to be Christ's witnesses and if we are to make disciples we need to know what a Christian is.

What a Christian is not!

Let us be clear about what a Christian is not. If we were to conduct a vox-pop by asking people (randomly) on the street the question, 'Are you a Christian?' we would probably get a variety of answers. There are several commonly held opinions as to what makes a person a Christian.

First, many people think they are Christians because they live (as much as possible) by keeping the Ten Commandments. They say they do the best they can. People who think like this believe a Christian is someone who is working hard to earn salvation. They think they deserve to be saved because of all the effort they have put into trying to be a good person. In short, they believe God rewards people who try to be good by granting them admittance into heaven. As such, they are the kind of self-righteous people Christ exposed as seriously deluded souls (Luke 18:9-12). They may be sincere but they are sincerely wrong.

A parable to illustrate

In the parable of 'The Pharisee and the tax collector' (Luke 18:9-14) we see two different kinds of men, two different approaches to God and two different outcomes. It is an ancient message which demands modern application. It has to be taken out of the 'then and there' and applied to the 'here and now'. It also needs to be taken out of the 'them and there' and applied to 'us and now'. This parable tells us something about the right and wrong way to approach God.

The Pharisee is a religious man who is unaware of his need for mercy. He belonged to an elitist group of experts in Judaic law. They were the theologians of their day. As custodians of truth they corrupted it by adding man-made regulations which became burdensome traditions imposed on people. Pharisees were the strictest sect of the day. They took pride in their piety and privileged position. They were prejudiced against Gentiles and Hebrew sinners. Furthermore, they were petty in their practice, dotting every 'i' and crossing every 't'.

On one occasion the chief priests and Pharisees sent temple guards to arrest Christ. But these guards returned without arresting Jesus. Asked why they had not done what they were instructed they replied, 'No one ever spoke like this man!' The Pharisees answered them, 'Have you also been deceived? Have any of the authorities or the Pharisees believed in him? But this crowd that does not know the law is accursed' (John 7:46-49). This incident reveals their contempt for ordinary people.

Unaware of his need for mercy

We encounter this Pharisee praying in the temple. He was there, possibly, out of a sense of duty. He would likely have been expected to be there. It appears that he was there to impress others and to earn favour with God. He focussed on the 'dos' and 'don'ts' of religion. He does not confess his sin. He seems completely unaware of his unworthiness. His greatest need is for mercy but he is ignorant of it as he prays about himself in what is an exercise in public self-congratulation.

This man's approach to God contrasts with that of Isaiah, 'Woe is me! For I am lost; for I am a man of unclean lips' (Isaiah 6:5). Isaiah was acutely aware of his sinful condition in the presence of the holy God. But this man recited the good things he does and the bad things he abstains from doing. His is a misplaced confidence in self-righteousness. Paul tells the Ephesians, 'For by grace you have been saved through faith. And this is not your own doing; it is the gift of God, not a result of works, so that no one may boast' (Ephesians 2:8-9).

If what this man said was true there was some degree of sacrifice in his religious observance. He did not steal (he said) but was he not at that very moment robbing God of the honour due to him? He says he does not commit adultery, but Christ taught that to look at a woman with lust was adulterous. How pure can any man's heart be in this regard? He says he is not an evildoer, but Scripture teaches that all have sinned and fallen short of the glory of God (Romans 3:23). He says that he fasts twice a week and gives a tenth of all he gets. But this sacrifice is offered to God in order to gain merit and so his approach is fatally flawed. There is also a degree of sincerity in his religion but he is sincerely wrong in his approach to God. This is true of much religion today that is characterized by sacrifice and sincerity.

Unconcerned about the tax collector

He expresses contempt rather than concern for the tax collector (or publican, AV). This lack of compassion is contrary to the heart of God. The Lord is, in his own words, 'merciful and gracious, slow to anger, and abounding in steadfast love and faithfulness, keeping steadfast love for thousands, forgiving iniquity and transgression and sin' (Exodus 34:6-7). The Pharisee refers to the tax collector in a manner intended to provide a contrast between his own righteousness and the sinfulness of this unworthy wretch! He did not compare himself to one of the great holy men of the Old Testament (even though they were all sinners) as this would have shown him in a less favourable light.

His criteria for measuring righteousness are relative. He compares himself to 'other men' and to 'this tax collector'. This comparison is a form self-deception. Many people today console themselves that they are not as bad as so-and-so. He has had an affair but I have been faithful to my wife. He has stolen things from work but I have been honest. He does not go to church but I always attend Sunday services. He does not give money to charity but I am on the charity committee and I tithe a tenth. He drinks alcohol but I abstain. He smokes and uses coarse language but I abstain from these. What the Pharisee did and abstained from doing was appropriate but not as a package offered to God to earn merit toward justification. Isaiah says, 'all our righteous deeds are like a polluted garment' (Isaiah 64:6). This being so, what are our sins like?

In weights and measures there are true standards by which we make judgments about the value of things, such as 2 lbs of sugar, 1 acre of farm land or a square yard of carpet. Imagine carpeting your home by guessing the length and width of the rooms. It cannot be a matter of speculation. A measuring instrument is required to ascertain the precise dimensions.

In evaluating our righteousness there is also a true standard; that standard is Jesus. There is no other standard. When measured against him we become conscious of our own unworthiness and our need of mercy. We also learn from this parable that our religion must be about a genuine relationship with God and characterized by compassion for sinners. Our concern should be evident in our prayers. In practice, people need to feel welcome rather than labelled, despised, excluded and rejected.

Unchanged when he leaves

Real encounters with God are life-transforming. They may not be dramatic but they move us closer to the mind and heart of God. The Pharisee went to a good place (the temple) and for a good reason (to pray). Many religious people today go to special buildings to pray but leave those places without having met with God. They are coming to God on their own terms seeking meritorious favour for their acts of righteousness and are ignorant of their greatest need, for mercy. James extends the gracious invitation, 'Draw near to God,' with the promise, 'and he will draw near to you' (James 4:8). This means drawing near to God on terms determined by him and that begins by appealing to his mercy.

The other man in this parable

First-century tax collectors in Palestine were generally ruthless as one would have to be to collect tax for the Roman occupying power. Their work involved other unpleasant duties such as repossessions, evictions and imprisoning poor defaulters. Many of them were extortionists who demanded more than was due, thus making their living by keeping the surplus. Many of them sub-contracted their responsibilities to others and became rich by obtaining a percentage from each of their sub-contractors. Thus unfortunate debtors often had to pay exorbitant additions to what they owed. Contractors would frequently engage sub-contractors from the localities where debtors lived. This local information helped contractors but made the tax collector a hated informer, traitor and instrument of oppression.

Pharisees taught their students not to associate with tax collectors because they were often in contact with Gentiles and worked on the Sabbath. This made them ritually unclean. This is one reason why they despised Jesus.

This tax collector 'stood at a distance'. This is not an insignificant phrase as it signifies that he was conscious of his unworthiness and sinful condition, and equally aware that God is holy. He stood at a distance because he recognized the immense distance between himself and God. He does not dare to look upward because he is ashamed of himself. His prayer was simple, 'God be merciful to me, a sinner.' It was not his humility that made him right with God but he approached God in humility on the basis of God's mercy alone. He did not seek to commend himself to God in unacceptable terms. He faced his sin and acknowledged his need of mercy. The Pharisee advertized his merit but the tax collector agonized for mercy and the outcome for both was completely different.

Spurgeon said, 'The publican was the best theologian — for he prays like David of old.' The events which inspired David's great penitential psalm (Psalm 51) are adultery and murder. He gratified his lust by committing adultery with Bathsheba. He arranged the killing of her husband, Uriah, who was a loyal and able warrior in the King's army. Thus we read these words, straight from the broken heart of God's anointed servant who had sinned and is now sorrowing: 'Have mercy upon me, O God, according to your unfailing love; according to your great compassion blot out my transgressions. Wash away all my iniquity and cleanse me from my sin. The sacrifices of God are a broken spirit; a broken and contrite heart, O God, you will not despise' (Psalm 51:1-2, 17, NIV).

By grace alone, through faith alone, in Christ alone

Many people today believe (wrongly) that they are Christians on the basis of what they do and don't do. They are asserting their right to be admitted into heaven on the basis of their own righteousness. This is an entirely wrong (unbiblical) approach to

God. Jesus made it clear that doing our best is not what makes a person a Christian (Luke 18:14). Our best is not good enough to get us into heaven.

If people care to look to God's Word to see what it has to say, they will find that salvation is by grace alone, through faith alone, in Christ alone. If we are willing to believe God's Word then there need be no confusion about what a Christian is. The Bible says that in God's sight 'all our righteous deeds are like a polluted garment' (Isaiah 64:6). This means that as far as God is concerned, even our best efforts (even the things we are most proud of), those things for which others have praised us, those things we are counting on to get us into heaven, are worthless. Hence, doing our best will not save us. Rather the Bible teaches that salvation is by God's grace, that is, unmerited favour.

Though it has already been cited it is worth stating again that Paul told the Ephesians, 'For by grace you have been saved through faith. And this is not your own doing; it is the gift of God, not a result of works, so that no one may boast' (Ephesians 2:8-9). On the positive side, these verses tell us that salvation is the free gift of God's grace. On the negative side they tell us our works have nothing to do with our salvation, and therefore nothing to do with how we become a Christian.[1] This is the consistent teaching of Scripture. Thus Titus may also be cited, 'he saved us, not because of works done by us in righteousness, but according to his own mercy, by the washing of regeneration and renewal of the Holy Spirit, whom he poured out on us richly through Jesus Christ our Saviour, so that being justified by his grace we might become heirs according to the hope of eternal life' (Titus 3:5-7). The bottom line is this: according to the Bible, trying as hard as we can to do the best we can is not what makes a person a Christian.

Popular ideas

If we return to the vox-pop I believe many people would say that they are Christians because their families have always been Christians. They might say their ancestors helped build this church building back in the 1740s (or whatever). They might say their parents and grandparents were members of the church. They might proudly boast that they have an uncle who is a pastor. People who give an answer like this believe that being a Christian is something you inherit. You are simply born into that tradition. It is a cultural assumption. In this regard they are like the Jews who said, 'We are offspring of Abraham', but Jesus said, 'You are of your father the devil' (John 8:31-47). Jesus made it clear that hereditary 'advantages' do not make us right with God.

For those who think that being a Christian is hereditary the Scripture says, 'But to all who did receive him, who believed in his name, he gave the right to become children of God, who were born, not of blood nor of the will of the flesh nor of the will of man, but of God' (John 1:12-13). These verses tell us that things like physical heritage, blood lineage, family connections or any other similar factors, have nothing to do with whether or not a person is a Christian. By God's grace, people who have come from pagan homes and false religions have professed faith in Christ and become Christians. On the other hand, there are people who have had the advantage of growing up in a Christian home who have rejected the gospel and died in their sins. So according to God's infallible Word heredity is not the determining factor as to whether or not a person is a Christian.

Then there are others who will say that they are Christians because they have always gone to church and Sunday school. People like this believe a Christian is someone who is involved in various religious activities. They might argue that they have been baptized and confirmed and their names are entered in the roll of membership. Thus they believe that one becomes a Christian when one undergoes certain religious rites and rituals. In this regard they are like Saul of Tarsus, who summarized the religious activities he engaged in prior to his conversion, saying, 'I was advancing in Judaism beyond many of my own age among my people, so extremely zealous was I for the traditions of my fathers' (Galatians 1:14). Elsewhere he says he was, 'circumcised on the eighth day, of the people of Israel, of the tribe of Benjamin, a Hebrew of Hebrews; as to the law, a Pharisee; as to zeal, a persecutor of the church; as to righteousness under the law, blameless' (Philippians 3:5-6). But when he becomes a Christian he gains a true spiritual perspective. Thus he goes on to say that in spite of all these religious activities he was not a Christian:

> *But whatever gain I had, I counted as loss for the sake of Christ. Indeed, I count everything as loss because of the surpassing worth of knowing Christ Jesus my Lord. For his sake I have suffered the loss of all things and count them as rubbish, in order that I may gain Christ and be found in him, not having a righteousness of my own that comes from the law, but that which comes through faith in Christ, the righteousness from God that depends on faith*
> (Philippians 3:7-9).

For those who think that a Christian is someone who is involved in various religious activities (or has gone through certain rites of the church) they should pay heed to what Jesus himself once said, 'On that day many will say to me, "Lord, Lord, did we not prophesy in your name, and cast out demons in your name, and do many mighty works in your name?" And then will I declare to them, "I never knew you; depart from me, you workers of lawlessness'" (Matthew 7:22-23). While Christians will certainly be involved in various religious activities, that involvement in and of itself, is not what makes a person a Christian.

I am sure some people would say, 'I know I'm a Christian because when the evangelist gave the invitation I went to the front of the auditorium. A counsellor had me pray a prayer, sign a card and date it, and then told me I had accepted Jesus as my Saviour. As a matter of fact, I've still got that card right here in my wallet.' While I'm not willing to discount the possibility some people have been saved under conditions similar to these, for those who have it is because the Holy Spirit enabled them to grasp the message of the gospel, and not because they went through certain motions. In other words, a person is not a Christian just because they walked the aisle, prayed the sinner's prayer, or signed a decision card. If this is what it means to be a Christian, we might as well say all the people who followed Jesus into Jerusalem waving palm branches and shouting, 'Hosanna!' must have been true disciples (John 12:12-15). Where were they when he was being crucified? Quite possibly many of them were the same people baying for his blood and choosing the release of Barabbas instead of Jesus!

For those who say that a Christian is someone who has done certain things (like walking the aisle at an evangelistic meeting, or praying a specific prayer or even going through a church's membership class and undergoing an examination by the elders of the church) the Scripture says, 'Now when he was in Jerusalem at the Passover Feast, many believed in his name when they saw the signs that he was doing. But Jesus on his part did not entrust himself to them, because he knew all people and needed no one to bear witness about man, for he himself knew what was in man' (John 2:23-25). Even though these people professed to believe in Jesus, he did not entrust himself to them because he knew their profession of faith was superficial. Thus according to Scripture, merely going through the motions of making a profession of faith does not ensure that a person has really become a Christian.

Then there is the person who says, 'I don't know if I'm a Christian or not, and I don't see how anyone can really know for sure in this life if they are going to heaven. So, I guess I'll just have to wait until I die to find out.' People who say this don't believe anyone can be sure (in this life) of a place in heaven hereafter. They might hope for heaven but they don't know for certain where they are going after death. Such people would probably think that people who say they do know they are going to heaven are being presumptuous. But Scripture clearly says the believer can know. John, writing to Christians, says, 'I write these things to you who believe in the name of the Son of God that you may know that you have eternal life' (1 John 5:13). The bottom line, then, is that Scripture clearly states that a person can know that he or she is a Christian, and can therefore have the assurance of salvation.

There are many common opinions regarding what constitutes a Christian. But most of them are not biblical. Some people think that all religions have the truth and that it does not matter which religion one belongs to. They think we are all walking different roads but all of them lead to the same place and what people believe is not that important, just as long as they are sincere. In other words, anyone whose religious beliefs are sincere is likely to go to heaven. People who take this position believe (wittingly or unwittingly) in universalism. This means they have embraced the self-contradictory belief that every religion contains truth and we will all eventually end up in heaven, regardless of the path we take to get there. But Scripture is absolutely clear that not everyone will go to heaven when they die. Jesus spoke of the resurrection to life and the resurrection to judgment (John 5:28-29).

The Bible says, 'Whoever believes in the Son has eternal life; whoever does not obey the Son shall not see life, but the wrath of God remains on him' (John 3:36). Jesus said that there will be a judgment, 'Then he will say to those on his left, "Depart from me, you cursed, into the eternal fire prepared for the devil and his angels"' (Matthew 25:41). He goes on to speak of how people will be separated on judgment day into the damned and the redeemed, 'And these will go away into eternal punishment, but the righteous into eternal life' (Matthew 25:46). Thus it is clear (according God's inerrant Word) that not everyone will go to heaven.

So there are many opinions about what a Christian is. But that is all they are, human opinions. We live in an age which believes that all opinions are valid. Today, truth is relative, so that people will say, 'What is true for you, does not necessarily have to be true for me'. In fact in our postmodern world people are permitted to hold completely contradictory views that are accepted as equally valid. The only absolute truth, they contend, is that there are no absolute truths, which in itself is a self-contradictory and inherently flawed way of thinking that undermines the credibility of such a philosophy or worldview.

When tested by the standard of God's Word these commonly held views about what a Christian is prove to be false, because they are at variance with what the Bible says. A Christian is not simply a person who does the best they can. A Christian is not simply a person who has been born into a religious home, whose parents are Christians, or who is active in a church. God has children but he does not have any grandchildren! Nor is a Christian simply someone who has been baptized or who has gone through the motions of responding to a gospel invitation. A Christian may do some of these things but doing them is not what makes him Christian.

A Christian is someone who has become aware of his sin, how awful it is, and therefore his own unworthiness in God's sight. A Christian is a person who has come to believe Jesus Christ is God's only provision for his sin, and therefore the only Saviour of sinners. A Christian is one who has repented of his sins and believed on the Lord Jesus Christ alone for his salvation and whose life, as a result of these things, has undergone (and continues to undergo) radical change, albeit solely and only by the grace and power of God.

Note

1. Certainly good works are expected of Christians and this is evident in the next verse in the same chapter of the letter to the Ephesians (Ephesians 2:10).

3

Defining a Christian

'And you were dead in the trespasses and sins in which you once walked ... and were by nature children of wrath, like the rest of mankind. But God, being rich in mercy, because of the great love with which he loved us ... made us alive together with Christ'

(Ephesians 2:1-5).

We have already seen that many people are confused by the word 'Christian'. They think they know what a Christian is. But if they were to compare their answer with Scripture they would discover they are wrong. Many people assume that knowing *about* Christ is the same thing as professing faith in Christ. They suppose all is well between themselves and God, when the truth is his eternal wrath still abides on them (John 3:36) because they have never repented of their sins, and had their sins forgiven (1 Corinthians 15:17).

We have seen that a person is not a Christian just because they are trying to be as good as they can. Obviously we expect Christians to be good people but that is not what makes a person a Christian. We have seen that the fact one's parents were Christians does not automatically mean one is a Christian. There are definite advantages to growing up in a Christian home, but that does not make a person a Christian. We expect Christians to attend worship and participate in certain ordinances like baptism and communion, but doing these things is not what makes a person a Christian.

What a Christian is

A Christian is someone who has become aware of his own unworthiness in God's sight. The level of awareness at the time of conversion will not be the same for everyone. Furthermore, our awareness of how unworthy we are prior to conversion might greatly increase after we are converted, as we become more familiar with what Scripture has to say.

First, a Christian is someone who has become aware of his unworthiness in God's sight due, in part, to the realization he is a sinner by practice. He recognizes he has broken God's laws more times than he can count and that he deserves to be condemned for what he has done. A Christian is able to identify with David's confession, 'Against you, you only, have I sinned and done what is evil in your sight' (Psalm 51:4). A Christian can identify with Isaiah who said, 'We have all become like one who is unclean, and all our righteous deeds are like a polluted garment' (Isaiah 64:6). A Christian can say with Paul, 'I know that nothing good dwells in me' (Romans 7:18). A Christian reads the story of the prodigal son, how he wandered away from his father, wasting his life and his resources in sinful living (Luke 15:11-13) and says, 'I was just like the prodigal son. I too wandered away from my heavenly Father. I too wasted the life God gave me in sinful, selfish pursuits!' A Christian reads the declaration made by John that, 'Everyone who sins breaks (God's) law' (1 John 3:4, NIV), and says, 'I have sinned against God because I have broken God's laws. I have broken the Commandments, so I am a sinner by practice.'

Second, a Christian is someone who has become aware of his own unworthiness in God's sight, in part, because he has also come to realize (perhaps not fully, but to some degree) that he is a sinner by nature. By God's grace, he has some measure of understanding that the nature with which he was born (that inner self) is in total rebellion against God and if it was not for God's restraining grace he would be capable of the worst sins imaginable. A Christian is someone who has come to God, saying with David, 'I was brought forth in iniquity, and in sin did my mother conceive me' (Psalm 51:5). A Christian can identify himself in the psalmist's words, 'The wicked are estranged from the womb; they go astray from birth' (Psalm 58:3). A Christian is one who understands that before conversion we 'were by nature children of wrath' (Ephesians 2:3).

Third, a Christian is someone who is not only concerned about his sinful behaviour, but also his sinful thoughts and desires. He recognizes the truth in Jeremiah's words that, 'The heart is deceitful above all things, and desperately sick' (Jeremiah 17:9). As believers we accept this as an accurate description of our natural condition. Christ's description of the unredeemed human heart reveals how defiled one is in an unregenerate state: 'For from within, out of the heart of man, come evil thoughts, sexual immorality, theft, murder, adultery, coveting, wickedness, deceit, sensuality, envy, slander, pride, foolishness. All these evil things come from within, and they defile a person' (Mark 7:21-23). Isaiah speaks of our human depravity, 'The whole head is sick, and the whole heart faint. From the sole of the foot even to the head, there is no soundness in it' (Isaiah 1:5b-6).

A Christian, then, is someone whose mind has been illuminated by the Holy Spirit, thereby enabling him to realize (in some measure) just how unworthy he is in God's sight; how undeserving he is of Christ's sacrifice on his behalf and how deserving he is of God's eternal wrath. In short, a Christian is someone who understands what Jesus really meant when he said, 'Those who are well have no need of a physician, but those who are sick. I have not come to call the righteous but sinners to repentance' (Luke 5:31-32).

The humanity and deity of Jesus

A Christian is someone who believes Jesus Christ is God come in human flesh and that as such he is the only Saviour of sinners and the only sacrifice for our sin. The full humanity of Jesus is affirmed throughout Scripture through the record of his birth (Luke 2:6-7), his life, and his death (John 19:30). Everything we go through, he went through. Everything we feel he felt, every temptation we face, he faced (Hebrews 2:18). He experienced hunger, thirst and fatigue (John 4:6-7). He felt love (John 13:23) and anger (Mark 3:5), joy and disappointment (John 14:9), pleasure and pain (Mark 15:15). An objective reading of the Gospel accounts of Jesus' life shows that he was a human being, with two exceptions: the manner in which he was conceived (Luke 1:34-35), and the fact that he never sinned (Hebrews 4:15).

The full deity of Jesus is also affirmed throughout Scripture. The Gospel of John opens by declaring that 'the Word was God' (John 1:1). The book of Hebrews says, 'He is the radiance of the glory of God and the exact imprint of his nature' (Hebrews 1:3). Jesus himself said, 'I and the Father are one.' Upon hearing this, unbelieving Jews picked up stones to stone him to death, 'for blasphemy, because you, being a man, make yourself God' (John 10:30-33). The miracles of Jesus attest to the reality that he is God (John 3:2). His teaching confirms he is God (Matthew 7:28-29). His sinless life verifies he is God (John 8:46). His resurrection from the dead testifies that he is God (John 10:18). Indeed, everything about him bears witness to the fact that he is God in human flesh.

A Christian, therefore, is a person who believes Jesus is both God and Man — even though we cannot fully understand how the divine nature and human nature have been joined together in Christ. It is impossible to be a Christian without believing these things because Scripture says, 'By this you know the Spirit of God: every spirit that confesses that Jesus Christ has come in the flesh is from God, and every spirit that does not confess Jesus is not from God' (1 John 4:2-3). To be a Christian, then, a person must believe Jesus is both fully God and fully man. He doesn't have to be able to unravel this mystery — but he does have to believe it.

In Christ alone

A Christian also believes this God-Man (Jesus) is the only Saviour of sinners, the only way to the Father, the only door to heaven, the only sacrifice for sin, the only means of salvation. He may not yet understand all the details of it but this one thing he believes, that, 'there is salvation in no one else, for there is no other name under heaven given among men by which we must be saved' (Acts 4:12). The Christian may not have a thorough grasp of systematic theology but he does know that, 'Christ Jesus came into the world to save sinners' (1 Timothy 1:15) and he identifies himself as such a sinner. Essentially a Christian is one who accepts the Bible as the inspired, inerrant and authoritative Word of God in all matters of faith and practice. He accepts Scripture as the revelation of God to humanity. He accepts what it says in relation to our origin as a species (creation), our purpose in life (to glorify God), our eternal destiny (heaven or hell) and the way of salvation (by grace alone, through faith alone, in Christ alone). The Christian relies on Christ alone for salvation and understands that, 'there is one God, and there is one mediator between God and men, the man Christ Jesus' (1 Timothy 2:5). The believer accepts that Jesus is the way, and the truth, and the life and that no one comes to the Father except through Christ (John 14:6).

To summarize, then, a Christian is someone who has come to believe Jesus Christ is both God and man united in one person. He believes that this God-Man, Jesus, is the only Saviour of sinners like himself. He accepts that apart from Jesus there is no other means of salvation, no other hope of eternal life, no other way to have his sins forgiven, no other possibility of getting into heaven and staying out of hell. In addition to these things, a Christian is also someone who has repented of his sins and believed on the Lord Jesus Christ. He recognizes God's grace as the means by which his sins are forgiven, and he receives the free gift of eternal life.

A new creation

Finally, a Christian is someone who has been changed by the power of God. A Christian is not the same person he was before conversion but like the apostle Paul he thinks and acts differently than he once did. So the Scripture says, 'Therefore, if anyone is in Christ, he is a new creation. The old has passed away; behold, the new has come' (2 Corinthians 5:17).

People ought to test their definition of what a Christian is against what the Bible says a Christian is. Don't take my word for it, find out for yourself. Be like the Bereans who 'received the word with all eagerness, examining the Scriptures daily to see if these things were so' (Acts 17:11).

The Word of God says, 'No one is good except God alone' (Mark 10:18). Scripture says, 'There is no one who does good, not even one' (Psalm 14:3). Scripture says, 'a person is not justified by the works of the Law but through faith in Christ Jesus' (Galatians 2:16). Many people believe that a Christian is someone who believes in God. A person who believes in God is a deist or theist but not necessarily a Christian. The devil is a deist and theist. The book of James says, 'You believe that God is one; you do well. Even the demons believe — and shudder!' (James 2:19). Certainly a Christian believes in God. But the true Christian believes in the God who has revealed himself in the pages of the Old and New Testaments (Isaiah 45:5-7). The real Christian believes in God as Creator (Romans 1:20). The genuine believer believes in God as the person of Jesus of Nazareth (Hebrews 1:3). But perhaps the clearest passage of all is found in 1 John 5: 'And this is the testimony, that God gave us eternal life, and this life is in his Son. Whoever has the Son has life; whoever does not have the Son of God does not have life' (vv. 11-12).

Repentance

Furthermore a Christian is someone who has actually repented of his sins and professed faith in Jesus Christ. In other words, by God's enabling grace, he didn't stop at believing the things just mentioned in some intellectual or theoretical way. A Christian is somebody who gives more than intellectual assent to those true doctrines which are based on a proper interpretation of Scripture. Rather the Christian is one who has not only been receptive to the truth but has actually responded positively to it by repenting of his sins and placing his trust in Jesus Christ alone for salvation.

In Scripture repentance always has to do with change. That means changing one's mind and behaviour. The prophet Jeremiah described how unwilling some people are to change their behaviour when he said, 'they refused to take correction. They have made their faces harder than rock; they have refused to repent' (Jeremiah 5:3). There are three crucial elements to true repentance.

First, true repentance means we are genuinely sorry for our sin. Biblical sorrow is not the same thing as being sorry we got caught. Nor is it the same thing as being sorry for any repercussions, consequences, or punishment we may have to face on account of what we have done. Instead, biblical sorrow has to do with being sorry for offending a holy and righteous God. This involves grieving over the fact we have displeased Almighty God. Thus it is the kind of sorrow that comes from knowing our sins have insulted our Creator and King to the point of justifiable outrage. The true penitent acknowledges that sin offends God. The Old Testament King David in his penitential prayer said, 'Against you, you only, have I sinned and done what is evil in your sight' (Psalm 51:4).

Second, true repentance involves genuine sorrow for what we are. Here there is an acceptance that we are sinful human beings by nature and by practice. When one encounters the living God the only appropriate response is like that of Isaiah, 'Woe is me! For I am lost; for I am a man of unclean lips, and I dwell in the midst of a people of unclean lips; for my eyes have seen the King, the LORD of hosts!' (Isaiah 6:5) Or like that of the tax collector in the temple who prayed, 'God, be merciful to me, a sinner!' (Luke 18:13). Or like Peter who once fell at Jesus' knees, and cried out, 'Depart from me, for I am a sinful man, O Lord' (Luke 5:8).

Third, true repentance also involves forsaking sin. This does not happen instantly, nor do we ever become perfect in this life. But real change takes place. So a Christian is not the same person he was before. He thinks differently and acts differently. The person converted to Christ knows that he is to be diligent about setting aside the old self and endeavour to put on the new self, which reflects the likeness of Christ (Ephesians 4:22-24).

Faith

Repentance is only one side of the coin. The other side is that a Christian is someone who has also professed faith in Christ or come to believe in the Lord Jesus (John 3:16; John 3:18; John 3:36). The person who believes in Christ has come to trust in or rely upon him alone for salvation. To put it another way, believing in Christ involves reliance. This may be illustrated by a patient who puts his life in a surgeon's hands by checking into the hospital and undergoing a scheduled operation, or an airline passenger who puts his life in a pilot's hands by getting on board the aeroplane.

So a Christian is someone who has put his eternal future and his hope of salvation in Jesus' hands by calling on him to forgive his sins (Psalm 32:5), save him from the wrath of God to come (John 3:36), give him the free gift of eternal life (Romans 6:23), and have a place waiting for him in heaven when this life on earth comes to an end (John 14:2-3). The glory of the gospel is that we are saved by grace alone, through faith alone in Christ alone. Augustus Toplady summed up the futility of offering anything to God in order to earn our salvation in the hymn, 'Rock of Ages':

> Not the labours of my hands
> Can fulfill Thy law's demands;
> Could my zeal no respite know,
> Could my tears forever flow,
> All for sin could not atone;
> Thou must save, and Thou alone.
>
> Nothing in my hands I bring,
> Simply to Thy cross I cling;
> Naked, come to Thee for dress,
> Helpless, look to Thee for grace;
> Foul, I to the Fountain fly;
> Wash me, Saviour, or I die.

4

Befriending sinners

'*The Son of Man came eating and drinking, and they say,
"Look at him! A glutton and a drunkard, a friend of tax
collectors and sinners!"'*

(Matthew 11:19).

Should a Christian have non-Christian friends? How many non-Christian people do you know? How many do you associate with on a regular basis? How many do you count as your friends? Better yet, how many non-Christian people consider you to be a friend? Jesus was rightly accused of being 'a friend of sinners'. The reality for many is that once a person becomes a Christian they lose contact with their unbelieving friends within a couple of years. Thus the Christian no longer has any significant relationships with non-Christians. This may be due in part to an intentional and necessary break with a past lifestyle. Peter identifies a former way of life from which believers have been redeemed and the tension that might arise when a convert ceases to engage in sinful activity. Thus he says, 'The time that is past suffices for doing what the Gentiles want to do, living in sensuality, passions, drunkenness, orgies, drinking parties, and lawless idolatry. With respect to this they are surprised when you do not join them in the same flood of debauchery, and they malign you' (1 Peter 4:3-4).

When a person becomes a Christian some of the leisure activities which once seemed like fun now seem to be distasteful and inappropriate. As a consequence the convert no longer spends as much time with his friends. When a person becomes a believer he has new interests, new ambitions and new attitudes. As a result of becoming a Christian, we begin to develop an interest in things we didn't care that much about before, like worship, reading and studying the Bible and talking about our faith. When we become believers we develop a new and healthy desire to be with like-minded people who share our passion for God expressed in corporate worship. The new believer is nurtured in an environment of meaningful spiritual fellowship.

The believer has a new nature. Paul says, 'Therefore, if anyone is in Christ, he is a new creation. The old has passed away; behold, the new has come' (2 Corinthians 5:17). So naturally we gravitate toward other Christians. Such newness of life might well be at variance with the way we once lived. Thus the believer will have a new interest in becoming a more honest employee, or a more faithful spouse and so on. Our interests change so that we become increasingly interested in spiritual matters, while our non-Christian friends are not interested in such things. So, a parting of the ways is normal and to be expected in certain circumstances. Hence, we begin to drift apart because we are no longer interested in many of the same things.

Another reason we may lose contact with non-Christians is due to a misinterpretation of Paul's words in 2 Corinthians where he said, 'Do not be unequally yoked with unbelievers. For what partnership has righteousness with lawlessness?

Or what fellowship has light with darkness? What accord has Christ with Belial? Or what portion does a believer share with an unbeliever?' (2 Corinthians 6:14-15). Some take this to mean we ought to cut off all contact with non-Christians or at least keep our dealings with them to a minimum. Hence, if we have a choice between hiring a Christian or non-Christian, we choose the Christian. If we have a choice between a Christian or non-Christian roommate, we choose the Christian. If we have a choice between doing business with a Christian and non-Christian, we choose the Christian. This is not necessarily a bad thing since Scripture says, 'Bad company ruins good morals' (1 Corinthians 15:33). But it does tend to isolate us from unbelievers, which is something Scripture never tells us to do. We are to be *in* the world but not *of* it. We are to be salt in a corrupt world and light in a dark world. Yet we create holy huddles which are no-go areas for unbelievers. We begin to think that church is a club for the holy rather than a fellowship of sinners redeemed by God's grace. We create enclaves that are like isolation units that quarantine us from any potential contaminating influence. There is a danger that such a church will be completely irrelevant. That is why evangelism and engagement needs to be examined by the church community in contemporary culture. Postmodern culture is more relational than rational, so winning the argument is less relevant and less likely to lead a person to faith than developing a relationship and befriending sinners.

Somebody once told me that he lived in Kenya for a time and was part of a church that was a gated community shut off from the outside world. Behind these security gates the body of believers worshipped God but had no contact whatsoever with the outside world. There was virtually no intersection of life where the opportunity of sharing the good news of the gospel was possible.

Paul's point about not being bound together with unbelievers is that we should never willingly yield control or influence over our behaviour, our moral decisions and our spiritual activities to an unbeliever by voluntary partnerships or associations. Paul told the Christians in Corinth, 'not to associate with sexually immoral people — not at all meaning the sexually immoral of this world, or the greedy and swindlers, or idolaters, since then you would need to go out of the world' (1 Corinthians 5:9-10). Clearly he did not say Christians should not have non-Christians friends. He simply warned us about becoming partners with unbelievers in their sinful practices and adopting their worldview. To put it another way, he was warning us about becoming like them by joining in their sinful lifestyle and sharing their system of belief. He was not telling us to avoid cultivating friendships with non-believers.

The Master is our model

Certain religious leaders had been saying that Jesus was a gluttonous man and a drunkard and a friend of sinners. Mark chapter two records that Jesus called a tax collector named Levi to be one of his disciples. Later on, Levi hosted a meal in his home that was not only attended by Jesus but also by many tax collectors and sinners. When the scribes and the Pharisees saw Jesus eating with such undesirables they asked his disciples, 'Why does he eat with tax collectors and sinners?' (Mark 2:13-16). Luke also records that both the Pharisees and the scribes grumbled about Jesus associating with such people (Luke 15:1-2). The scribes and Pharisees were separatists and couldn't image anyone socializing with a group of sinners (like Jesus did) without being a sinner himself.

On the other hand, many of the tax-collectors and sinners would have seen Jesus' willingness to eat with them as a gesture of friendship, not an endorsement of their sinful lifestyles. They would have known from his teaching and behaviour that he did not do the things they did. But the fact he was willing to socialize with them indicated that he was sincerely interested in them. The scribes and Pharisees contemptuously accused Jesus of compromising his integrity by such unwholesome associations. They spoke these words with an attitude of superiority borne out of a religious attitude rooted in cultural assumptions.

Jesus was neither a glutton nor a drunkard. Scripture tells us that drunkenness and gluttony are sins (Proverbs 23:20; Deuteronomy 21:20). It also tells us Jesus was without sin (Hebrews 4:15). Hence, he could not possibly have been a glutton or a drunkard. Perhaps many of these religious leaders knew the accusation was not true. I suspect they were being spiteful and knowingly slandered Jesus. I assume they were angry and frustrated with Jesus because he was so willing to associate with people they found so offensive. But essentially they were self-righteous religious snobs. Nevertheless their accusation that Jesus was a friend of tax collectors and sinners was true, proving that even a stopped clock is right twice a day!

It has already been pointed out in a previous chapter that many of the tax collectors to whom the scribes and Pharisees referred were Jews who collected monies from their own people on behalf of the hated Roman government. It was made clear there that anything they could collect above what Rome required was theirs to keep and that this is how they made their living. We need to remind ourselves again that they were considered unscrupulous traitors, partly because they feathered their own nests at the expense of their fellow countrymen. They were deemed to be unclean because they had contact with Gentiles and indeed some of them were Gentiles. Not only did Jesus eat socially with tax collectors like Zacchaeus (Luke 19:1-10) but he actually chose a tax collector (Levi/Matthew) as one of his twelve apostles (Matthew 9:9).

The Pharisees used the word 'sinner' as a kind of generic term to describe anyone who did not follow their extra-biblical traditions. On one occasion Pharisees and scribes witnessed Christ's disciples eating bread with unwashed hands. This was a breach of the Judaic custom diligently observed by the Pharisees (*cf*. Mark 7:1-4). A similar example is found in Luke 11 where a Pharisee asked Jesus to dine with him. Jesus went to this man's home and reclined at the table. The Pharisee was shocked that Jesus had not first ceremonially washed before the meal. This earned the rebuke from the Lord, 'Now you Pharisees cleanse the outside of the cup and of the dish, but inside you are full of greed and wickedness' (Luke 11:37-39). Clearly Jesus even socialized with religious bigots.

Not everyone the Pharisees labelled 'sinners' were of the notorious variety but some had apparently established notoriety in the community. Some of the tax collectors he spent time with really were corrupt, greedy cheats. They were extortionists. Some of the women Jesus associated with were prostitutes (Luke 7:37-39). Some of the other people he ate and drank with were social outcasts. It is likely that many of these people were coarse and ill-mannered. They were probably rough, uneducated, crude, and hardened by sin and life's troubles. They were probably not the nicest or most pleasant people to be around. But Jesus ate with them. They were not cultured or refined but Jesus mingled with them. They were not genteel or sophisticated but Jesus deliberately spent time with them. If the Master is to be our model in all things then he must be our model in this example. All that he did was intentional and has purpose and significance.

Befriending sinners

I used to work on a special education programme for disadvantaged youth. The purpose was to provide a structured educational programme to compensate these young people for their lack of attainment in the formal, second level school system. Many of them had social problems and difficult home environments. It was a community-based programme and I was the director. In this role I came in contact with many of the parents, mostly mothers. I would summon them from time to time to discuss the welfare of their children. Some of these women were prostitutes. They would occasionally call to my office uninvited to advocate on behalf of a child who was expelled from school and was wandering the streets, getting into trouble. They wanted to know if I could help. Over time I built up a positive relationship with people in the community, including these women. Then one evening my wife and I were going to a piano recital by a world famous Christian pianist at a venue in the city centre. It was the kind of occasion where one made a special effort to dress up, so we were both in formal evening wear. The area where the concert hall was situated was close to a red-light district frequented by soliciting prostitutes and their clients. When we arrived outside the hall all the parking spaces had been taken and there was a queue of Christian people waiting to gain access to the building. Eventually I found a parking space and as my wife and I walked from the car and approached the queue several ladies of ill repute emerged from the shadows and hailed me enthusiastically by name! They were scantily clad in a manner that clearly indicated the profession to which they belonged. They repeatedly called out my name and I sheepishly waved at them and they laughed. Many people waiting to gain entry to the concert hall turned and looked at me. It was clear that these women knew me by name. I wasn't ashamed to know them in the way I did but I was embarrassed that others might misunderstand. I blushed and my wife blushed too! I sometimes think of that incident whenever I read about Jesus the friend of sinners and it makes me smile.

The friendship that Jesus extended to sinners was genuine. He was not pretending to be a friend of tax collectors and sinners. He really was their friend. His friendship did not have any strings attached to it. He was not feigning friendship in order to gain their confidence so he could carry out some other agenda. He really did care about these people. In fact, he cared about them regardless of whether they responded to his teaching or not (Mark 10:17-22). Like the Samaritan in Christ's parable who came upon a man on the road to Jericho who had been beaten, robbed and left for dead (a man none of the religious people would stop and help), Jesus felt compassion for sinners. This motivated him to get involved in their lives (Luke 10:30-33).

Unlike the prodigal son's older brother, who wanted nothing to do with his wayward sibling after he squandered his inheritance in wild living (Luke 15:13), Jesus felt compassion for sinners and lovingly embraced them with his friendship (Luke 15:20).

It is important to add, though, that while Jesus' friendship was genuine, there was also a specific purpose behind his being a friend of sinners. It was not what we would call an 'ulterior motive'. That would have been a form of deception. Rather, it was part of a divine strategy for finding and saving his lost sheep. So when certain religious leaders grumbled about Jesus eating and drinking with tax collectors and sinners, he said, 'Those who are well have no need of a physician, but those who are sick. I have not come to call the righteous but sinners to repentance' (Luke 5:30-32). To put it another way, Jesus did not become a friend of tax collectors and sinners to show the religious leaders how broad-minded he was, or how narrow-minded they were. Nor did he do it to show people he was just an ordinary guy. Rather, Jesus did it to draw them to himself in repentance and faith. Here Jesus is exemplary. This, too, is our calling. It cannot be otherwise. It is the Jesus of the Gospels that we are called to model ourselves upon. To use a fishing analogy (which is a biblical analogy): to catch fish you have to go where the fish are. Jesus was fishing for sinners so he went where the sinners were, and became their friend.

If we use the physician analogy (which is also a biblical analogy), a doctor who spends all his time with healthy people, and never gets involved with the sick, is not doing his job. Jesus came to save those who are spiritually sick, so he went where the sick people were. He came to save his lost sheep, so he went out looking for them (Luke 15:1-7). He came to save sinners, so he befriended them. And yet his friendship was genuine. He really did care about them. He never withdrew his friendship because they refused to repent and profess faith in him. Jesus continued to befriend sinners up to the day he went to the cross. In his dying hour he reached out to the repentant thief and promised him paradise. Jesus is still the friend of sinners today. He does not love their sin. He does not condone the bad things they do. If Jesus was not willing to befriend sinners none of us would ever have been saved.

Developing friendships with non-Christians

It is clear from the foregoing discussion that Jesus was a friend of sinners. The question is, are we and if not, why not? Some would argue (as we have already discussed) that Scripture teaches us to keep ourselves separate (1 Corinthians 15:33; 2 Corinthians 6:14, 17). People who think like this will undoubtedly have their arsenal of Scripture texts to defend their position. They might cite James 4:4 which says: 'Do you not know that friendship with the world is enmity with God? Therefore whoever wishes to be a friend of the world makes himself an enemy of God', and 1 Corinthians 5:6: 'Do you not know that a little leaven leavens the whole lump?' Of course each passage has to be taken in context, especially since some of the ones just quoted actually have more to do with matters within the church than making friends with non-believers. Nevertheless, the danger is real. Hence, when building friendships with non-Christians we have to be careful not to get drawn into their world to the point where we start imitating their lifestyle and adopting their worldview.

Potential danger, however, is no excuse not to look for ways to build friendships with non-Christians. Paul said, in a passage quoted earlier, 'not to associate with sexually immoral people — not at all meaning the sexually immoral of this world, or the greedy and swindlers, or idolaters, since then you would need to go out of the world' (1 Corinthians 5:9-10). Here Paul is talking about not associating with believers who are living promiscuous lives. He is not ruling out association with the sexually immoral of this world, or the greedy, swindlers, and idolaters. The implication is that we may rightly associate with such people. In this instance, the Greek word for 'associate' means 'to mingle, to mix up with, and/or to keep company with'. Hence, it signifies more than just a passing, superficial relationship. It actually refers to people we spend time with! Why would Scripture tell us to spend time with swindlers, and idolaters, and various other kinds of immoral people? There can only be one reason — so our friendship might become the means for seeing some of them come to Christ!

The challenge for us is that since Jesus was known as 'a friend of tax collectors and sinners' then we too by his enabling grace need to make a conscious effort to build some friendships with non-Christians. We need to look around and see who the Lord might be leading us to build a friendship with. Maybe we can befriend a co-worker, or a neighbour, someone we do business with, or someone in the club or organization we belong to. If we are not already doing so we need to start making an effort. We need to take time to talk with them. We need to ask questions. We should find out what they are interested in and find out what is going on in their lives. We need to invite them to lunch or to a movie or have them over for coffee or dinner. If they need something we have, we should offer it. If they need sympathy, we should give it. If they need to be encouraged, we need to encourage them.

We don't need to worry initially about sharing our faith, or saying something 'spiritual' or even inviting them to church. Obviously, if they open the door by asking us a direct question, then we should go for it. But that is not the goal to begin with. The goal is to be a friend. The aim is to build genuine friendship that will continue even if we never get to share the gospel with them. Our friendship should be of such a quality that it will endure difficulty. The goal is to be like Jesus, who became known as 'a friend of tax collectors and sinners' because he took the time to eat with them and just be with them. He took the initiative, now we must do likewise.

5

Relational evangelism

'One of the two who heard John speak and followed Jesus was Andrew, Simon Peter's brother. He first found his own brother Simon and said to him, "We have found the Messiah"... The next day Jesus decided to go to Galilee. He found Philip and said to him, "Follow me."... Philip found Nathanael and said to him, "We have found him of whom Moses in the Law and also the prophets wrote, Jesus of Nazareth, the son of Joseph." Nathanael said to him, "Can anything good come out of Nazareth?" Philip said to him, "Come and see"'

(John 1:40-46).

Here we see relational evangelism in operation. Before our Saviour ascended back to heaven he gave us a mandate to be his witnesses (Acts 1:8). But we cannot possibly carry it out unless we have both the desire and the ability to do so. Therefore, we must humbly ask God to enable us. The Holy Spirit will enable us to fulfil this mandate. We must be conscious of the fact that the fields are ready to be harvested, but the labourers are few (Matthew 9:37). We must ask the Lord of the harvest to send out workers (Matthew 9:38). It is in fulfilling the Master's mandate that our profession of faith and love is verified by our obedience to his command (James 1:22; John 14:15).

Finding an approach that fits

After the great Chicago fire in 1871, D. L. Moody became one of the first evangelists to use the altar call in evangelistic meetings. From that day to this, many have criticized this method of evangelism, where people are invited, begged or cajoled to profess faith in Christ by raising their hand, walking to the front of an auditorium to talk with a counsellor, and kneel to pray. The story is told of a pastor who once took Mr Moody to task for this practice. After listening to his objections, the evangelist said: 'I agree with you, brother. I don't altogether like the method myself, and I'm always looking for a better one. What's yours?' The minister was surprised by the question, and had to admit he did not invite people to profess faith in Christ as Saviour. Upon hearing this Mr Moody said, 'In that case, I like my method better than yours.'

There are many different methods of evangelism, such as 'altar calls', handing out tracts, preaching evangelistic messages, knocking on doors, and trying to build friendships with non-believers. So what method do we use? I have engaged in street preaching, door-to-door cold-calling, preached evangelistic sermons in church services, distributed tracts on the street and from house to house, taught introductory courses to the Bible for non-believers (such as *Christianity Explored*). I have witnessed to individuals (friends, family members, work colleagues and so on). I have used the 'cover' of a questionnaire/survey to try and get a foot in someone's door. I have given Bibles and Christian books away. I have written gospel books as evangelistic tools. I have preached to my congregation the importance and urgency of evangelism and witnessing, thereby spurring them on to engage in evangelism and witnessing for Christ. I have helped to train evangelism teams. Some of these methods have worked better than others. I am more comfortable with some ways and not so comfortable with others. Over time I have learned what works best for me. I have found a method that fits. What works well for me might not work for you but I believe we must find some means that is right for us as individuals and for each church.

Evangelism might be left to the evangelism team but witnessing is the responsibility of all believers. If we don't like one method, which one do we like? What method are we actually using as part of a strategy to fulfil Jesus' mandate? If we are not using any then we are failing in our sacred duty and that is a matter that needs to change. No one method of evangelism is going to fit everyone. Hence, we need to be cautious about criticizing methods we don't use and don't like. We also need to be careful about criticizing people who don't use the methods we use.

When David was preparing to go and fight Goliath he was still just a young shepherd. Scripture recounts how King Saul clothed David in his armour:

> *Then Saul clothed David with his armour. He put a helmet of bronze on his head and clothed him with a coat of mail, and David strapped his sword over his armour. And he tried in vain to go, for he had not tested them. Then David said to Saul, 'I cannot go with these, for I have not tested them.' So David put them off. Then he took his staff in his hand and chose five smooth stones from the brook and put them in his shepherd's pouch. His sling was in his hand, and he approached the Philistine*
>
> (1 Samuel 17:38-40).

The fact is some people find that certain methods of evangelism are a lot like trying to wear someone else's armour. It may work for others, but it doesn't work for them. Some find a particular method effective and useful but others find it awkward and ill-fitting. Indeed, it may actually hinder them from fulfilling the mandate to be witnesses for Christ. There is much missional activity today which comes into this category. We should praise God some people can use this method and that method if people are coming to Christ as a result.

But what method fits us, our spiritual gifts or our natural abilities or God-given personality? Instead of being critical about this and decrying the potential dilution or pollution of the gospel, we need to pray and ask the Lord to show us a method of evangelism that fits us; instead of using the lame excuse that we don't have the gift of evangelism (most people don't) and doing nothing, we need to find a method that works for who we are and how God has made us.

The importance of relationships

You may have noticed that several people became disciples of Christ in the verses quoted at the top of this chapter, including Andrew, Simon, Philip and Nathanael. When we examine this passage for clues as to how these men came to follow Christ, we find that they had a significant relationship with someone whom God used to bring them to the Saviour. For John and Andrew that someone was John the Baptist, their mentor and teacher. For Peter that someone was Andrew, his brother. For Nathanael that someone turned out to be his friend, Philip. That leaves Philip whom Jesus appears to have personally found and called directly to himself without using a mentor, or brother, or friend (John 1:43). This underscores the fact that, while our Saviour often uses our relationships with other people to draw them to himself in repentance and faith, he is not ultimately dependent on us. The fact he often uses us is a matter of grace, rather than necessity. It is a privilege he grants to us.

Three ways

When it comes to evangelism there are different ways of sharing our faith. Most methods of evangelism will fall into one of these three categories. All three are legitimate and by God's grace all three have been effective to varying degrees. However, few (if any) people will find that all three of these methods fit them.

The first of these methods is preaching. This form of 'proclamation evangelism' is thought by many today to be outmoded and irrelevant. This is a mistake. The Word of God will never be void of power. The words of Isaiah need to be borne in mind: 'For as the rain and the snow come down from heaven and do not return there but water the earth, making it bring forth and sprout, giving seed to the sower and bread to the eater, so shall my word be that goes out from my mouth; it shall not return to me empty, but it shall accomplish that which I purpose, and shall succeed in the thing for which I sent it' (Isaiah 55:10-11). Paul instructs Timothy to 'preach the word; be ready in season and out of season; reprove, rebuke, and exhort, with complete patience and teaching' (2 Timothy 4:2). Jesus was a preacher. If he is to be our model we cannot ignore this. Mark records:

Now after John was arrested, Jesus came into Galilee, proclaiming the gospel of God, and saying, 'The time is fulfilled, and the kingdom of God is at hand; repent and believe in the gospel'

(Mark 1:14-15).

The church must have confidence in the divine power of the Word of God to search the heart, bring conviction of sin and quicken the soul in repentance. The writer to the Hebrews presents us with the fact that God's Word is an effective means of communicating the message of the gospel: 'For the word of God is living and active, sharper than any two-edged sword, piercing to the division of soul and of spirit, of joints and of marrow, and discerning the thoughts and intentions of the heart' (Hebrews 4:12).

When we talk about presenting the gospel through preaching we are talking about preaching the true gospel and not one of the inaccurate or watered-down versions that are often proclaimed today. It is clear from the book of Acts that preaching was central to the spread of the gospel. Proclamation evangelism is carried out today whenever a pastor preaches the gospel of Jesus Christ from the pulpit on Sunday. God uses preaching to draw people to himself:

> *How are they to call on him in whom they have not believed? And how are they to believe in him of whom they have never heard? And how are they to hear without someone preaching? And how are they to preach unless they are sent? As it is written, 'How beautiful are the feet of those who preach the good news!'*
>
> (Romans 10:14-15).

Of course not every believer is gifted by God to be a preacher of the gospel. Most Christians will not be able to fulfil Christ's mandate to be his witnesses by preaching.

The second way of sharing our faith is what might be called 'confrontational evangelism'. This essentially consists of targeting people and trying to share the gospel with them, often in a relatively short amount of time. In John's Gospel, chapter four, Jesus engaged the Samaritan woman at the well in such a way. In Acts chapter eight Philip came upon an Ethiopian eunuch sitting in his chariot, parked alongside a desert road, reading from the book of Isaiah. Philip approached the man and asked if he understood what he was reading (Acts 8:30). A conversation ensued that eventually led to the man professing faith in Christ and being baptized.

Today this method of evangelism is often associated with activities like knocking on doors or witnessing to the person seated next to us on the bus, train or aeroplane, or striking up a conversation with people in a variety of locations. Though evangelists will be quite happy with this approach, many Christians are uncomfortable with this way of sharing their faith. Many believers who would be happy to share their faith at a meeting to which non-Christians are invited will cringe with embarrassment or recoil in fear at the thought of approaching (intruding uninvited in the lives of) strangers. Many Christians are willing to share their faith with strangers in such situations if the stranger initiates the conversation or asks a question about the believer's faith but feel uncomfortable about taking the initiative themselves. Frequently time constraints in such contexts means that only a truncated version of the gospel can be conveyed and one wonders if such an approach alienates more people than it endears to the message of the gospel.

I am not saying this way of communicating the gospel should be forsaken but I am saying that it is not suitable for all believers. Many Christians would be too nervous and would feel that such an approach contravenes social etiquette. I know that some people will contend that such sensitivities should be set aside for the sake of the gospel but what we are trying to do here is reflect on the means of evangelism. We are seeking to consider the different ways of sharing our faith with a view to finding some approach that works. Individuals differ in personality. Some are extroverts and others are introverts. Some are bold while others are shy. We should not try to impose a method of evangelism on people who do not have that gift but we must all try to find a way that works.

Most Christians want to share their faith. It is natural. There are times when it is right for believers to move out of their comfort zones to speak about Jesus. But generally we all want to find a means of witnessing that is more in keeping with the gifts and personality God has given to us. Working outside your comfort zone ultimately leads to anxiety, stress and burnout.

Thus we come to the third way of sharing our faith which we will call 'relational evangelism'. As the term suggests, this method essentially consists of building relationships with people before we share the gospel of Jesus Christ with them. It has also been called 'friendship evangelism' or 'lifestyle evangelism'. Jesus was a relationship builder. He spent much time eating and drinking, and otherwise socializing with lost people (Luke 15:1-2). It was this relational approach to evangelism that earned Jesus a reputation for being a friend of sinners.

Contemporary approaches to evangelism tend to emphasize the relational method and there are many workshops and seminars specifically designed to train and encourage people to adopt a relational approach to disseminating the message of the gospel. Developing relationships with our non-Christian colleagues will eventually lead to significant opportunities for witnessing. I think we need to be careful about our integrity in this regard. I would not like to think that a Mormon or Jehovah's Witness colleague was befriending me (e.g. helping me to move my furniture to my new home) for such ulterior motives. Yet many Christians are being encouraged to engage in this kind of subterfuge. Ultimately trust is built on honesty and openness.

It is difficult for any church to quantify witnessing of this kind, as distinct from evangelism on Wednesday evenings from 7.00pm to 9.00pm, for instance. Those who engage in this sort of activity are genuinely seeking to fulfil Christ's mandate to be his witnesses. If we are motivated by love for the lost we will want to reach out and help them in whatever way possible. This is how we earn the right to be heard. Certainly the age of 'megaphone diplomacy', that is, shouting out the message of the gospel on street corners, is no longer as effective in Western culture (or perhaps in any culture) as it was a generation ago. It is far more likely that the Christian will have opportunity to share his faith in the context of a caring relationship that has been built over time. This is time-consuming. Notwithstanding the reservations expressed, I think, on the whole, this method of witnessing is to be commended. It is better than pressing people whom we do not know to receive Christ immediately when we do not have any meaningful kind of relationship with them. Relational evangelism is preferable to rushing people through a stripped down version of the gospel because there is not enough time to explain it comprehensively.

From weaklings to witnesses

After the crucifixion of Jesus the disciples were huddled together behind locked doors because they were afraid (John 20:19). Later however, after the risen Lord appeared to them, they were filled with boldness and went about proclaiming the gospel. They were transformed from weaklings to witnesses. We also need such a transformation. We often huddle together in our church buildings and home Bible study and prayer groups. Our doors are not bolted shut but perhaps we have a siege mentality. The enemy is out there and we are safe in here! Certainly the church is to be engaged in fellowship, prayer and the study of Scripture, the breaking of bread and worship (Acts 2:42). But it is also to be involved in making disciples (Matthew 28:19) and bearing witness for Christ (Acts 1:8). If we are honest we must confess that we are often frightened by this prospect and prefer the safety of our little (or perhaps large) groups.

Our Saviour's example indicates that we Christians need to learn how to be 'in the world' (John 17:11), without being 'of the world' (John 17:16). We need to learn how to befriend sinners without becoming compromised or contaminated. This will involve getting our hands dirty but keeping our hearts clean. We need to learn how to 'be separate' (2 Corinthians 6:17) without becoming 'separatists' (Acts 10:28). We need to learn how to devote ourselves to the apostles' teaching and to fellowship, to the breaking of bread and to prayer (Acts 2:42), without cutting off all meaningful contact with lost people who don't share our appreciation for such things. To put it another way, we need to learn how to keep our conduct among those outside the church honourable (1 Peter 2:12).

Why Christians should socialize with non-Christians

Why should we socialize with non-Christians? Some of them use foul language, tell vulgar jokes, and take our Saviour's name in vain. Many of them have a different set of moral values than we do. For example, many of them don't see anything wrong with things like adultery, homosexuality and, perhaps, abortion. They obviously don't love God, Christ, and his Church the way we do. Do we consider them to be a potentially contaminating influence because some of them smoke, drink alcohol, dance, and go to X-rated movies? Some of them cheat on their income tax, their expense account, and their husband or wife. Given these and other differences, why would we Christians want to socialize with them? Why make the effort? Why take risks? Should we not just protect and preserve what we have? The answer is that Jesus is our role model and he befriended sinners.

Scripture repeatedly tells us to imitate our Saviour (Ephesians 5:1, for example). We might not be able to follow his example perfectly, we will not be able to imitate him in an area in which we have not been gifted (such as preaching), but with regard to befriending sinners we can and indeed must imitate our Lord. Everything Jesus did was instructive. In spending time with sinners he taught his disciples that they too ought to associate with the non-religious, those in false religions, the profane, the despised, the marginalized and the rejected. Often they were slow to learn the lessons he sought to teach them so that, some time after Jesus had returned to heaven, Peter was still hesitant to associate with Gentiles because of his Jewish upbringing. Indeed, in Acts chapter ten it took a special vision from God, along with a voice from heaven, before he would go to the house of a Roman centurion named Cornelius and preach the gospel (Acts 10:9-48; 11:1-18). Still later, on yet another occasion, Paul had to rebuke Peter for refusing to eat with Gentiles because Peter was afraid of what certain Jews might think (Galatians 2:11-21).

Peer pressure is a reality in the lives of believers! Objections, resistance and condemnation often come from our fellow believers who misunderstand and wrongly judge our activity. Christians are essentially conservative people. But Jesus was radical and subversive. He subverted people's expectations and upset the religious establishment. If we seek to do evangelism in a different way we will soon encounter the knee-jerk reaction of those who want us to conform to the tried and trusted methods of the past. Many such methods are good and should not be jettisoned for the sake of novelty. Opposition may come from within the church and even (perhaps, especially) from the top. Many leaders are in maintenance mode rather than mission mode. That is one of the reasons why many missional people today will lead mission activity 'under the radar', so to speak, that is, without the official sanction or support of the local church to which they belong.

Christians should associate with non-Christians so that they can build relationships and friendships in the hope of eventually getting opportunity to share the gospel. We need to leave the comfort and safety of our Christian enclaves because Jesus came to call sinners to repentance and he desires to use us to do it. The gospel is about Christ Jesus coming into the world to save sinners (1 Timothy 1:15).

The Pharisees were highly trained, religious people. Indeed their outward spirituality would put many of us to shame. They were faithful about things like prayer, and tithing, and worship. Moreover, they studied God's Word and tried to obey his laws. And yet they lacked love and compassion, especially for those in most need of God's mercy, like the tax collectors and sinners. Religious leaders like the Pharisees should have been exemplifying God's love and forgiveness to tax collectors and sinners by associating with them and seeking to assist them spiritually. Instead they kept themselves separate.

If we isolate ourselves from non-Christians and stay in our Christian clubs (churches) and if we don't make the effort to associate and build friendships with lost people then God will be offended by everything else we do, including the things his

Word commands us to do. Our prayers will be profitless, our worship will be worthless and our fellowship will be a farce (Matthew 23:23).

Why should we leave the comfort and safety of our churches and go and befriend sinners? One reason is because we have been commanded to do so. How are we going to fulfil the Great Commission to 'go … and make disciples of all the nations' (Matthew 28:19) if we do not get out and associate with non-Christians? If we stay in our holy huddles they will not come to us. How are we going to fulfil our Saviour's mandate to be his witnesses (Acts 1:8) if we don't go to the 'Jerusalems', and 'Judeas', and 'Samarias' of the world? How can we be a 'physician's assistant' to the sick if we don't spend time with the sick (Matthew 9:12)? How can we catch fish if we don't go where the fish are (Matthew 4:19)?

Jesus did not spend all his time with tax collectors and sinners but he spent enough to be scornfully accused of being their friend. Christ has left an example for his disciples to follow in his steps (1 Peter 2:21). God graciously uses people like us to lead others to salvation. He chooses to use us despite all the problems involved in doing so. In fact, it is likely he receives more glory by working through weak creatures like us to accomplish his redemptive purposes (2 Corinthians 12:9). Scripture says that some plant, others water and still others get to reap the harvest (1 Corinthians 3:6-9) but everyone has a role. So everyone needs to be out in the field working (Matthew 9:37) because that is ordinarily the way people are saved.

People are lost in their sins and need to be found (Luke 15:1-32). Other biblical metaphors tell us the unsaved are dead in their trespasses and sins, and need to be regenerated in newness of life (Ephesians 2:1), or that people are enslaved to sin (John 8:34) and need to be set free. Jesus said, 'For the Son of Man came to seek and to save the lost' (Luke 19:10). That's what we should be doing also.

But the most sobering reason of all for evangelism and engagement with the non-Christian is that they are on their way to a lost eternity unless they repent of their sin and profess faith in Christ. The idea that people outside of Christ are inexorably doomed to spend eternity in hell is not politically correct but it is what the Bible says (Matthew 25:41). If the church is going to declare the whole counsel of God (Acts 20:27) it must address this matter.

Saved from what?

R. C. Sproul tells the story of being unexpectedly confronted by a young man on a college campus who, without so much as a 'Hello', blocked his path and asked: 'Are you saved?' Sproul says even though he knew what the young man meant, he was startled by the question and before he could think, blurted back: 'Saved from what?' At which point a puzzled look came over the young man's face and after several moments of silence the young man simply turned around and walked away, without answering Dr Sproul's question.

As a Christian, have you ever thought about what it is you have been saved from? One common evangelical answer is that we have been 'saved from our sins'. But what exactly does that mean? Does it mean we are saved from ever sinning again? Such false notions are based on the misinterpretation of certain passages of Scripture (like Romans 7:15-19; and 1 John 2:1). It means that the believer is saved from the ultimate power of sin. As such the Christian is no longer a slave to sin, as he was before coming to Christ (Romans 6:11-14; and 1 John 3:9-10). The one who puts his trust in Jesus is saved from the ultimate penalty of sin. Physical death is certainly one part of that penalty which all people (Christians and non-Christians alike) must undergo (Genesis 2:16-17; Hebrews 9:27). But spiritual death is another part of that penalty (Romans 6:23; Ephesians 2:1) and the Christian is saved from that consequence because Jesus has atoned for his sin at Calvary. Spiritual death is separation from God. This definition of spiritual death is inadequate. The non-Christian may errantly reason that if that is the worst thing that happens to him when he dies it won't be so bad, especially since he never had much interest in God anyway.

The Bible teaches that non-believers are already separated from God before they die (Ephesians 2:12). To say the penalty of sin is separation from God after death is a misleading understatement. It is a statement that needs to be explained more fully. Separation from God is God's way of exercising just retribution on unrepentant sinners. The unredeemed are standing directly in the path of the storm of God's righteous anger. Therefore, the correct answer to the question 'Saved from what?' is that, thanks to Jesus Christ, the believer has been saved from ever having to experience God's wrath on account of his sins. If the seriousness of the situation is underestimated it will inevitably result in a casual attitude to evangelistic engagement with non-Christians.

No sin goes unpunished, not even the sins of the redeemed. Certain verses of the New Testament speak of 'propitiation' (Romans 3:24-25; 1 John 4:10). This theological word means 'to appease, to placate, or to pacify'. God's wrath against us on account of our sins has been propitiated by Christ's sacrifice. Instead of pouring out his wrath on us, God poured it out on Christ as he hung on the cross. Thus, our sins have not gone unpunished; rather Jesus was punished in our place. As a result, justice has been served. God's holiness remains intact and God has been glorified through the demonstration of his wrath against sin (Romans 9:22). Those who have believed in the Son of God have escaped. God's wrath no longer abides on the one who has believed in the Son of God. Instead, they have received the free gift of eternal life (John 3:36). But the person who does not believe in Jesus will not inherit the eternal life of bliss that awaits the redeemed. Not only that, but the wrath of God abides on him (John 3:36).

Some cults, like the Jehovah's Witnesses, attempt to escape God's wrath by teaching a doctrine known as annihilation: that there is no life after death for the lost, they simply cease to exist. Sadly this idea has crept into some Christian churches that deny the existence of hell. Hell needs to be preached from the pulpit. If this is neglected it will impact negatively on the importance and urgency of evangelism. It will result in undermining Christian witness. Scripture has a great deal to say about God's wrath, judgment, and hell. A study of any Bible concordance will show anyone interested in the truth that there are as many references in Scripture to the anger, fury and wrath of God as there are to his grace, and love, and tenderness.

Furthermore, Jesus spoke vividly of the reality of hell and of the terribleness of God's wrath: 'Depart from me, you cursed, into the eternal fire prepared for the devil and his angels' (Matthew 25:41). Jesus warned: 'fear him who, after he has killed, has authority to cast into hell' (Luke 12:5). In fact Jesus spoke more often about hell than about heaven.

The subject of God's wrath is not confined solely to the Old Testament (as some would like us to believe). It is also spoken of in the New Testament. Hence, in addition to the passages cited above (from the Gospels of Matthew and Luke) Paul, writing to the Thessalonians, said: '...when the Lord Jesus is revealed from heaven with his mighty angels in flaming fire, inflicting vengeance on those who do not know God and on those who do not obey the gospel of our Lord Jesus. They will suffer the punishment of eternal destruction, away from the presence of the Lord and from the glory of his might...' (2 Thessalonians 1:7-9). The apostle John also speaks of God's wrath in a vivid manner: 'Then the kings of the earth and the great ones and the generals and the rich and the powerful, and everyone, slave and free, hid themselves in the caves and among the rocks of the mountains, calling to the mountains and rocks, "Fall on us and hide us from the face of him who is seated on the throne, and from the wrath of the Lamb, for the great day of their wrath has come, and who can stand?"' (Revelation 6:16-17). The theme of God's wrath permeates Scripture. We should not be silent about this when the Bible is so vocal about it. The gospel is not good news without it for how will people ever understand the seriousness of their spiritual condition and the urgency and importance of being saved unless they have some understanding of what it is they need to be saved from?

God's wrath is directed at sinners. The evangelical cliché that 'God hates sin but loves sinners' is inaccurate and misleading. It is not the sin of immorality that will be cast into hell, but the sinner whose immorality goes unforgiven. It is not the act of murder that will experience the fierceness of God's wrath but the person who has committed murder and who dies with his sin, unrepentant. It is not a person's lies that will face God's righteous anger, but the person whose lies have not been forgiven. Hence, Scripture says: 'But as for the cowardly, the faithless, the detestable, as for murderers, the sexually immoral, sorcerers, idolaters, and all liars, their portion will be in the lake that burns with fire and sulfur, which is the second death'

(Revelation 21:8). How blessed, then, is that man or woman whose sins are forgiven. As the Scripture says, 'Blessed is the one whose transgression is forgiven, whose sin is covered. Blessed is the man against whom the LORD counts no iniquity' (Psalm 32:1-2). For the redeemed God has imputed the righteousness of Jesus Christ to their account. In that happy condition, in Christ, there is no condemnation (Romans 8:1). But many in the church today are asleep on this matter and need to be awakened from their slumber.

6
Let's go fishing!

'Follow me, and I will make you fishers of men'
(Matthew 4:19).

Jesus invited Peter and his brother Andrew to follow him, promising to make them fishers of men. Shortly thereafter he extended the same invitation to James and his brother John (Matthew 4:21). For most people, fishing is a leisure activity. It is something they do on vacation or at weekends as a form of recreation and relaxation. As such it is something they do for fun. But for these four men it was their occupation and that makes their immediate response all the more notable. Christ called them to be his disciples but he also called them to the work of evangelism. Henceforth they were to be his witnesses. By describing that task as fishing for men, Jesus used a figure of speech all four men could easily understand. It is an interesting metaphor Jesus used to connect with these men.

Today, given the fact that so many people have computers connected to the internet Jesus might have said, 'Follow me, and I will show you how to surf for men.'[1] Had he been talking to businessmen, he might have said, 'Follow me, and I will use you to bring clients into my kingdom.' Had he had been talking to members of a search and rescue team, he might have said, 'Follow me, and I will show you how to search for and rescue people who are lost in their sins'. Had he been talking to firemen he might have said, 'Follow me and I will make you rescue souls from the fires of hell.' None of these attempts to modernize the call captures the simplicity or symbolism of our Saviour's words quite so well. Most people have some idea of what it means to go fishing. Therefore, let us examine the Saviour's fishing metaphor to see what light it may shine on the mandate to be his witnesses.

Three methods of fishing

Three methods of fishing were used at the time of Christ in first-century Palestine. One is angling, which involved a hook and line, similar to how most recreational fishermen fish today. Jesus referred to this kind of fishing in one incident:

> When they came to Capernaum, the collectors of the two-drachma tax went up to Peter and said, 'Does your teacher not pay the tax?' He said, 'Yes.' And when he came into the house, Jesus spoke to him first, saying, 'What do you think, Simon? From whom do kings of the earth take toll or tax? From their sons or from others?' And when he said, 'From others,' Jesus said to him, 'Then the sons are free. However, not to give offence to them, go to the sea and cast a hook and take the first fish that comes up, and when you open its mouth you will find a shekel. Take that and give it to them for me and for yourself'

> (Matthew 17:24-27).

Let's go fishing!

But this is not the kind of fishing Jesus had in mind when he said, 'Follow me, and I will make you fishers of men.' A second way of fishing involved a large net strung between two or more boats. This was usually used in deep water. This may be the kind of fishing Jesus had in mind when he said,

> 'Again, the kingdom of heaven is like a net that was thrown into the sea and gathered fish of every kind. When it was full, men drew it ashore and sat down and sorted the good into containers but threw away the bad. So it will be at the close of the age. The angels will come out and separate the evil from the righteous and throw them into the fiery furnace. In that place there will be weeping and gnashing of teeth'
>
> (Matthew 13:47-50).

In some ways this is a picture of what we call the 'visible church'. Many churches have people among their congregations who are true Christians (i.e. 'good fish') as well as people who think they are Christians but are not (i.e. 'bad fish'). Therefore, all of us should make sure that we really belong to Christ (2 Corinthians 13:5).

We have to be one of Christ's redeemed people before we can be one of his witnesses. And the only way we become one of his people is by admitting we need a Saviour, repenting of our sins and professing faith in Jesus as the only Saviour of sinners like ourselves (John 20:31; Acts 20:21). Afterwards, as proof that our conversion to Christ was genuine, we are to strive to obey his commands (John 14:15), albeit not in our own strength, but by his power, otherwise we will just be playing church and deceiving ourselves (James 1:22).

A third method of fishing used in Jesus' day involved a different kind of net — one usually thrown from shallow water along the shore. Matthew used the Greek word for this kind of fishing: 'While walking by the Sea of Galilee, he saw two brothers, Simon (who is called Peter) and Andrew his brother, casting a net into the sea, for they were fishermen' (Matthew 4:18). Here the phrase 'casting a net [*amphibion*] into the sea' is the word from which the English word 'amphibious' or 'amphibian' is derived. These words describe animals or plants that can live on land and/or in water, and also certain dual-purpose vehicles that function on both land and water.

This is the kind of fishing Peter and Andrew were doing when Jesus called to them and said, 'Follow me, and I will make you fishers of men.' So we might paraphrase Christ's words like this: 'Follow me, and I will teach you how to cast your net for souls.' Matthew used a different word for 'net' in verse twenty when he said Peter and Andrew, 'Immediately they left their nets and followed him' (Matthew 4:20). The word here is *diktuon*. Again in verse twenty-one the word he uses for nets is *diktuon*: 'And going on from there he saw two other brothers, James the son of Zebedee and John his brother, in the boat with Zebedee their father, mending their nets, and he called them' (Matthew 4:21). This is a general word that could refer to any kind of net, including nets to catch birds or animals. Obviously, in this context they were fishing nets.

Net fishing is not a leisurely pursuit like angling. It is hard work (Luke 5:5). If you are fishing from the shore you have to learn how to throw your net correctly, so it covers as large an area as possible. This requires both instruction from somebody experienced as well as a considerable amount of practice. In the same way we need to learn how to throw the net of the gospel correctly, otherwise, the likelihood of catching anything will be remote. Moreover, it is helpful if we have someone to teach us. And we need to practise if we are going to master the technique.

Let's go fishing!

Net fishing requires us to repeatedly throw our nets into the water and then draw them in to see if we have caught anything.

In a similar fashion, we cannot be content to periodically throw the net of the gospel into the sea of lost men every year or so. We have to keep at it. We have to be willing to do it over and over if we expect to see any significant results. We have to keep throwing the net out and drawing it in, again and again and again.

A second thing net-fishing implies (especially the kind where a net is strung between two or more boats) is that ordinarily the work of evangelism ought to be carried out as a cooperative rather than an individual effort. Jesus told Simon (Peter) to 'Put out into the deep and let down your nets for a catch' (Luke 5:4). Peter answered: 'Master, we toiled all night and took nothing! But at your word I will let down the nets' (v. 5). Luke then goes on to say: 'And when they had done this, they enclosed a large number of fish, and their nets were breaking. They signalled to their partners in the other boat to come and help them. And they came and filled both the boats, so that they began to sink' (vv. 6-7). This is a job that requires team effort. That does not mean everyone will be doing the same thing. Forgive me for mixing metaphors, but Paul once said: 'I planted, Apollos watered, but God gave the growth. So neither he who plants nor he who waters is anything, but only God who gives the growth. He who plants and he who waters are one, and each will receive his wages according to his labour' (1 Corinthians 3:6-8). He also said (to mix metaphors even further): 'I laid a foundation, and someone else is building upon it' (1 Corinthians 3:10). Some plant the seed of the gospel in people's lives, some water it, others cultivate it, and eventually (if God wills) someone else gets to harvest it. Likewise, someone lays the foundation of the gospel in a non-Christian's life, someone else comes along and builds on it, someone else comes along and builds on it some more, and finally (by God's grace) someone else gets to cut the ribbon at the official opening ceremony for that building!

It is worth noting that Paul viewed those who supported him financially and/or prayed for him regularly as co-workers in his efforts to spread the gospel of Jesus Christ (2 Corinthians 9:13; Philippians 4:15). Jesus instructed his disciples to be his witnesses and such endeavour does not mean working independently of, or in competition with each other. Rather it ought to be a coordinated body effort (1 Corinthians 12:12) where each member has a role to play.

Two basic fishing principles

Regardless of the method, there are at least two principles that apply to all kinds of fishing. First, a fisherman has to go where the fish are. Fish live in an environment that is totally different from ours. They will not come to us because they cannot live in our environment. So if we are going to have any chance of catching some of them we are going to have to go where they are. Non-Christians live in a world very different from ours. This means they are not going to feel comfortable coming to us, so we are going to have to be willing to enter their world. That is why it is important to start trying to build relationships with non-believers. We need to get to know them in their environment, to spend time with them in surroundings they find comfortable. We need to try to draw them into our 'nets' of friendship and love before introducing them to the world of the church, which is strange to them.

Many people are not interested in fishing, so they don't go fishing. They don't own any fishing tackle and so they don't even consider going fishing. Many Christians have the same problem when it comes to fishing for souls. They are not really interested in doing it so they don't, hence the sad fact that some Christians have not had a part in anyone coming to Christ in twenty, thirty, or forty years! Some Christians have never led anybody to Christ. Indeed, many believers are not actually equipped to get involved. It really does not matter whether I go fishing for fish or not. But it matters a great deal whether or not I'm involved in fishing for souls. It matters because Jesus expects us to be his witnesses (Acts 1:8). It matters because people are lost in their sins and need to be found (Luke 19:10). It matters because God's eternal wrath hangs over the head of every non-Christian (John 3:36). Jesus invited us to follow him and he promised to make us fishers of men. Jesus can equip us for the task.

The other basic principle is that no one fisherman catches all the fish, nor does any fisherman land every fish he sets out to catch. Every true fisherman has a tale about 'the one that got away', the one that snapped his line, slipped off the hook, or escaped through a hole in his net. Every fisherman has a tale about the 'big one' in the lake — the one that's been there for years (that people see from time to time) but no one has ever been able to catch.

In a similar fashion, even the best witness for Christ will not be able to manoeuvre every fish into his net. Not every non-Christian we try and build a relationship with will respond in the way we might like. Not every non-Christian we try to make friends with will want to be friends with us. Not every non-Christian with whom we become friends will respond to the gospel in repentance and faith.

Such setbacks never stop a true fisherman because he knows there are other fish he will catch. Likewise, any setbacks we encounter as we go about fulfilling the mandate to be Christ's witnesses (and there will be setbacks) should not stop us from continuing to pursue Christ's calling to be fishers of men. God is sovereign and he decides who will be saved. That means we will catch those he has determined for us to catch. Those whom he has ordained to be caught will be caught. Those whom he has predestined to find their way into our net will find their way into our net. Hence Scripture says that as Paul and Barnabas preached the gospel in the city of Pisidian in Antioch, 'as many as were appointed to eternal life believed' (Acts 13:48). Knowing this encourages us to keep throwing the net of the gospel into the sea of unsaved souls and drawing it in because we know God has ordained that we will catch some. So let us keep fishing and leave the results to him.

The compassion of Christ

Matthew records Jesus' reaction on one occasion: 'When he saw the crowds, he had compassion for them, because they were harassed and helpless, like sheep without a shepherd' (Matthew 9:36). God is compassionate (Deuteronomy 4:31). Jesus, being the radiance of God's glory and the exact representation of his nature (Hebrews 1:3), often felt compassion (Matthew 14:14) for people on account of their physical sicknesses and spiritual plight. We can be thankful to God that he is compassionate to us even though we had offended him with our sins (Habakkuk 1:13). Even when we were his enemies, Jesus felt such a deep sense of compassion for us that he gave his life on the cross so we would not have to face judgment. As followers of Jesus we ought to feel some measure of compassion for those around us who are still lost in their sins. But if we are honest we will have to admit that often we don't. If God has turned our hearts of stone into hearts of flesh (Ezekiel 36:26) we should not be cold and indifferent about the lost.

Imitating the Saviour's example

Once Jesus Christ becomes our Saviour, he then becomes our example in all things. He is the one whose speech, behaviour, and way of thinking we are to imitate. He is the one whose pattern we are to follow as we go about living our lives. For instance, having washed the disciples' feet, Jesus told them to imitate his example of humility and servitude, saying, 'For I have given you an example, that you also should do just as I have done to you' (John 13:15). The apostle Peter told believers to imitate Jesus' example (1 Peter 2:21-23). The apostle Paul told Christians to 'be imitators of God' in love (Ephesians 5:1). Luke reminds us to imitate Christ's mercy (Luke 6:36). Jesus exhorted his disciples to 'pray earnestly to the Lord of the harvest to send out labourers into his harvest' (Matthew 9:38). Are we doing that?

What caused Jesus to give up his divine form and take on the form of a man (Philippians 2:6-7)? What motivated him to leave heaven, and come to earth so that he could teach and preach, mingle with and heal sinful people? Why did Jesus voluntarily suffer the pain, humiliation and death of the cross (John 10:17-18)? Why did he endure the agony of separation from God the Father (reflected in the words, 'My God, my God, why have you forsaken me?' — Matthew 27:46)? He did it because he loved us (Romans 5:8). It was an act of tremendous mercy and grace (Hebrews 8:12; Ephesians 2:5). He had compassion for the lost and if we are going to be like him we must not only speak his words and imitate his actions but we must also feel Christlike compassion for sinners.

Imitating Christ's compassion

The Greek word for 'compassion' (*splanchna*) used here refers to a person's bowels, intestines or other internal organs. It is sometimes used that way literally, as it is to describe the death of Judas for example (Acts 1:18). But more often it is used figuratively to refer to a person's emotions, much like we might use the word 'heart' today. The word compassion used by Matthew to describe how Jesus felt stresses the depth and intensity of Jesus' emotions. Thus we see the extent and strength of his sympathy. Jesus is deeply concerned for the people around him.

It is instructive to note how often the word 'compassion' is used to describe how Jesus felt about the people around him. After the execution of John the Baptist, Jesus took a boat to a secluded place so he could be alone (presumably to grieve) but a crowd followed him. Matthew records: 'he saw a great crowd, and he had compassion on them' (Matthew 14:13-14).

On another occasion Jesus miraculously fed several thousand people who had been following him using seven loaves of bread and a few fish, because, he said, 'I have compassion on the crowd because they have been with me now three days and have nothing to eat. And I am unwilling to send them away hungry, lest they faint on the way' (Matthew 15:32).

Another time, as Jesus was leaving Jericho, two blind men cried out: 'Lord, have mercy on us, Son of David!' So Jesus stopped and asked them what they wanted. They replied, 'Lord, let our eyes be opened...' at which point Scripture says, 'And Jesus in pity touched their eyes, and immediately they recovered their sight and followed him' (Matthew 20:29-34).

On yet another occasion, a leper approached Jesus, fell on his knees and said, 'If you will, you can make me clean.' Mark records the evident response of Jesus to this man's predicament and earnest plea: 'Moved with pity, he stretched out his hand and touched him and said to him, "I will; be clean." And immediately the leprosy left him, and he was made clean' (Mark 1:40-42).

Again, as Jesus was approaching the city of Nain, he encountered a funeral procession coming out the city gate carrying the dead body of a widow's only son. Luke says, 'And when the Lord saw her, he had compassion on her and said to her, "Do not weep." Then he came up and touched the bier, and the bearers stood still. And he said, "Young man, I say to you, arise." And the dead man sat up and began to speak, and Jesus gave him to his mother' (Luke 7:11-15).

It is important to realize that Jesus' compassion for people went beyond their need for things like food and healing. He did not overlook these needs but he saw an infinitely greater need in people's lives — one that far surpassed hungry stomachs and sick bodies — one that was even more important than restoring blind eyes or raising the dead. There is no doubt Jesus felt compassion for people because of their physical needs but he felt even greater compassion for them on account of their spiritual needs. In fact, the physical miracles Jesus did, which people could easily see, were often done to show them he could also take care of their spiritual needs which were not as easy to see (Matthew 9:2-6). When Jesus looked at the multitudes, he did not just see blind eyes. He saw their spiritual blindness, their alienation from God, their enslavement to sin.

Lots of people feel some measure of compassion for the plight of others but they never do anything about it. Not so with Jesus. His compassion always resulted in action. He always did something to help people in need — whether it was healing their infirmities, teaching them what God's Word really meant (Matthew 5:21-48), or preaching the gospel of salvation through faith in him (Matthew 9:35). Sometimes we can be moved emotionally by the needs of others without being moved to action. We may feel sorry for people on account of their situation, but not enough to do something about it. We might sympathize with their predicament, but not enough to actually try and help.

To put it in biblical terms, we are many times more like the priest and Levite, who passed by the man on the Jericho road who had been robbed and beaten, when we should be like the Samaritan. Scripture says he 'had compassion' for him, and then translated that compassion into action by treating and bandaging his wounds and providing him with shelter at his own expense (Luke 10:25-37).

I once heard a story about students at a theological seminary who were about to sit an important examination set by one of their professors. On the approach road to the seminary building where the examination hall was situated a man lay in the street with blood on his face and clothes, and he was asking passers by for help. The students passed by, one by one, in a hurry to sit the paper. Some stepped over him and others stepped off the sidewalk to avoid him. When they arrived in the examination hall and were seated the exam papers were distributed. There was only one question: 'Discuss the meaning of the Parable of the Good Samaritan.' A note below the question explained that 10% would be allocated for a good exposition of the parable and 90% for lending assistance to the man in the street. The professor had arranged for that man to position himself in the path of the students attending the exam. The blood on his face and clothes was not real but appeared to be so. As the students looked in horror at the paper and then in embarrassment at one another the door to the exam hall opened and a student arrived fifteen minutes late. He took his seat and when he saw the paper his face lit up. He had stopped to lend assistance to the man in the street. He looked at the professor at the top of the room and the professor returned a smile. He alone passed that exam.

Let's go fishing!

The point of this story is obvious. We can know much about compassion in theory but unless we practise it we fail miserably.

Let us get practical. Someone we know is in the hospital or nursing home, but we don't go visit them because we don't like those kinds of places. Someone we know is struggling with depression but we don't go out of our way to talk with them to see how they are doing because depressed people make us feel depressed. Someone we know is grieving over the death of a spouse but we don't go and offer comfort because we don't like talking about death. It is not just the pastor's job to do these things! Someone we know is lost in their trespasses and sins, but we don't try and build a friendship (in the hope of being able to share the gospel with them at some point in the future) because we are too busy and don't want to get that involved in someone else's life. Compassion that is not transformed into some kind of action is worthless.

With regard to the crowds that gathered around Jesus, anyone could see the physical needs these people had because their poverty and sickness were evident. But Jesus could also see the deeper needs many of these same people had. Many of these people probably did not even know they had deeper, spiritual needs. Jesus was not deceived by their outward religious appearance. He saw their hearts (Jeremiah 17:9-10). He saw them like sheep without a shepherd and he was deeply moved. The people were 'harassed' and 'helpless'. Other versions of the Bible (we are using the ESV) translate this in different ways. The idea is that these people were weary and scattered, dispirited and distressed. The idea being conveyed is that these people were worn out to the point of total exhaustion and were utterly helpless.

There is also inherent in this a severe rebuke to the religious leaders of the day for being false shepherds who did not take care of the people's spiritual needs. Instead of feeling compassion for the people they were supposed to be shepherding, the scribes and Pharisees were largely responsible for the distress which people felt.

Today there are still religious leaders who are diluting and distorting God's Word and causing people to become spiritually distressed. One way this is done is by telling people 'a good God would never condemn anyone to hell', thereby leading them to believe they don't need to repent of their sin and profess faith in Jesus Christ. Another way people are discouraged is by telling them they can work their way into God's favour by avoiding certain sins, performing good deeds, and going through certain religious rites, ceremonies and rituals. Thus people are led to believe that all this talk about sin, and the need for repentance, and the need to trust in Jesus Christ alone for their salvation is just a lot of nonsense.

Jesus feels compassion for people like this and if we are going to fulfil the mandate to be his witnesses, we need to feel compassion for them too. Jesus not only feels compassion for sinners like drug addicts and drunks, prostitutes, murders and thieves but he also feels compassion for 'religious sinners' — i.e. for people who have been deceived into thinking they are in good standing with God, when the truth is they are still as lost in their sins as anyone can be. Many people have an outward veneer of religion, they are what we might call 'good people' (from a superficial and human perspective) but in reality they are still lost because they have never repented of their sin and made a genuine profession of faith in Jesus Christ. Jesus feels compassion for people like this too and so should we if we truly are his disciples.

We do not always feel compassion for the lost people around us, be they irreligious or religious. Nor can we simply just turn on the compassion switch. We do not grieve over them as we ought. So let us begin by confessing that indifference, and heartlessness, and selfishness, and ask the Lord to give us a genuine, heart-felt, Christlike compassion for the lost people living around us. This is a necessary prerequisite for every individual member of the church community in contemporary culture if we are to move toward effective evangelism and engagement today.

If we were to expel people from the church for failing to make an effort to fulfil the Great Commission to 'Go and make disciples' how full would our churches be or how empty would they become? We discipline people for failing to make an effort to comply with the commands of Scripture in other areas of life. I'm not advocating it but I think it is an interesting thought that makes us reflect on what we tend to prioritize and what we feel is crucially important or relatively unimportant.

Loving the lost and lonely

At times of sorrow, grief and loneliness it is comforting to know that there is someone to whom we can turn; one who under-stands. In the prophetic portrait of Isaiah 53 Jesus is described as 'a man of sorrows'. Sorrow is an inescapable part of life. Sorrow was an intrinsic part of the purpose of his mission: Christ came to bear our sorrows. We have confidence in his ability to comfort those who are sorrowing because we are aware of his authentic experience and consequent capacity for empathy.

Rejection

Let us examine the sorrows of Christ. Firstly, there is the sorrow of rejection: 'He was despised and rejected by men; a man of sorrows, and acquainted with grief' (Isaiah 53:3). Rejection brings the deepest of sorrows. His love was rejected. His truth was rejected. His kingdom was rejected. He was rejected by his people: 'He came to his own, and his own people did not receive him' (John 1:11). He was rejected by those in his home area:

> ...and coming to his hometown he taught them in their synagogue, so that they were astonished, and said, 'Where did this man get this wisdom and these mighty works? Is not this the carpenter's son? Is not his mother called Mary? And are not his brothers James and Joseph and Simon and Judas? And are not all his sisters with us? Where then did this man get all these things?' And they took offence at him. But Jesus said to them, 'A prophet is not without honour except in his hometown and in his own household.' And he did not do many mighty works there, because of their unbelief
> (Matthew 13:54-58).

He was rejected by the crowd at the cross along with the religious leaders: 'And those who passed by derided him, wagging their heads... So also the chief priests, with the scribes and elders, mocked him' (Matthew 27:39-41).

Jesus cares about those who have suffered the sorrow of rejection. As individual believers and as a church we need to be careful not to reject others. Christ befriended sinners but we tend to avoid 'bad company' for fear of contamination or fear of losing our respectable reputations. We are to be *in* the world but not *of* it and we are to be a holy people, set apart for Christ. Have we come to interpret this as the theological justification for a kind of religious apartheid? Jesus was not segregated from sinners. Have our churches become quarantine centres where the holy congregate and the unholy feel unwelcome?

How many of us would have qualms about our church buildings being used as centres to address social issues in our communities? Why is the church not in the front line in addressing the social scourge of drug addiction or providing places of refuge for battered women? Could the local church be more involved in offering compensatory education programmes for the disadvantaged? Surely there is scope for the provision of support services, such as marriage counselling, as well as strategic outreach programmes to the excluded, without capitulating to the 'social gospel'.

Grief

Secondly, there is the sorrow of grief. Isaiah 53:3 identifies Christ as one who was familiar with grief. We are all acquainted with suffering. This is part of the fallen human condition whereby tears are common to us all. People experience the grief of shattered dreams; the grief of broken homes; the grief of witnessing the suffering experience by loved ones; the grief of losing loved ones in death. Our Lord is 'acquainted with grief'. He did not insulate himself from grief — he cried at the grave of Lazarus. When he saw his friends sorrowing he was moved to tears (John 11:33-35). He shed tears for Jerusalem (Luke 19:41). How much of this compassion do we demonstrate for those crushed with grief? Incarnate Christian living demands such Christlikeness.

Christ enters into our grief and we must enter into the sorrows of the lost and lonely. We can bring our deepest grief to Jesus. He waits at the throne of grace. He provides grace to help in the time of need (Hebrews 4:16). His grace is sufficient for our grief (2 Corinthians 12:9).

Loneliness

Thirdly, there is the sorrow of loneliness, 'as one from whom men hide their faces he was despised, and we esteemed him not' (Isaiah 53:3). He walked that lonely road for you and me. He prayed in Gethsemane alone (Luke 22:40-46). At his arrest, his disciples deserted him and fled (Matthew 26:56). He stood before the high priest alone (Luke 22:63-68). He was tried before Pilate alone (Luke 23). That sense of loneliness is captured in the anguished cry from the cross: 'My God, my God, why have you forsaken me?' (Matthew 27:46). But he will not forsake his disciples (Matthew 28:20; John 14:18; Hebrews 13:5). How privileged we are as believers, to have Jesus to comfort, support, encourage and befriend us.

In today's societies there is a great deal of loneliness. One does not have to live in isolated rural locations to feel lonely. On the contrary it is often most keenly felt in densely populated urban centres where individualism has led to estrangement in once tight-knit communities. The social infrastructure of previous generations is rapidly disappearing, leaving in its wake many who are becoming increasingly marginalized, alienated and disillusioned. I am aware of a secular-run volunteer programme where volunteers visit the elderly and lonely simply to befriend them. How has the church allowed such a vacuum to exist? It seems that the only voices calling out 'Stop!' to corporate greed are radical, secular activists. Where are the Christian voices in these campaigns? Perhaps we tend to see them as the loony fringe because we have become part of the establishment.

People need to know that God longs to take the burdens of grief and loneliness and place them in relationships that are supportive and loving; not least with his Son, the Lord Jesus Christ. Let those of us who have accepted his comfort share this good news with the rejected, grieving and lonely people in our society. Let us love the lost and lonely as Jesus loves them. A true church is not just an elitist cohort of biblically literate people who engage in quaint rituals. Rather it is a community where people are led to faith, wholeness and maturity in Christ.

It would be nice to say that the Christian church is distinguished as a community of people who have exchanged their grief for gladness, their rejection for acceptance and their loneliness for love. But it is not true, and we cannot promote Christianity on that basis. However, we can be a people who know gladness even in grief, acceptance (by Christ) in spite of rejection by others and love in times of loneliness. Jesus was a person who experienced grief, rejection and loneliness. But Jesus was a person who loved the broken-hearted and the excluded. As his ambassadors we ought to be a people who love the lost and lonely. We cannot invite people to exchange their grief for gladness but we can tell them that in the darkest hour of sorrow they can know the comfort of Christ. We cannot invite people to exchange their rejection for acceptance but we can tell them that even if others reject them that Jesus will not. We cannot invite people to exchange their loneliness for love but we can tell them that even in the midst of loneliness there is one who loves them deeply.

Prayer for evangelism

'Then he said to his disciples, "The harvest is plentiful, but the labourers are few; therefore pray earnestly to the Lord of the harvest to send out labourers into his harvest"' (Matthew 9:37-38). Our Lord is worthy of our adoration and worship, our reverence and love, and last but not least, our obedience (Psalm 2:11; Revelation 4:11; John 14:15). God's Word instructs us to pray (1 Thessalonians 5:17), Jesus taught his disciples how to pray (Luke 11:1-4), and his Word gives us some specific examples of prayers offered by his people. Yet Scripture is right when it says, 'we do not know what to pray for as we ought' (Romans 8:26). Part of the reason for this is because when we do pray we often focus on many of the less important matters of life, while neglecting weightier issues (Matthew 23:23). Our Saviour taught us to pray for everyday matters under the phrase 'our daily bread' (Matthew 6:11) but he also told us to beseech the Lord of the harvest to send out workers into his harvest (Matthew 9:38). We must confess we do the former quite often and the latter far less, if at all. Therefore we need to be persuaded of the importance of praying for harvest workers.

Prayer is an essential and integral part of evangelism. It has already been noted that Paul frequently asked other Christians to pray for him. He did not ask for safe travel or comfort (not that it is wrong to ask for these things). Rather, he asked other believers to pray that he would be a faithful witness for Jesus so that the gospel might prosper and the Lord be glorified. Even when Paul did ask for prayer for personal issues, like being released from prison (Philemon 1:22), it was not so he could be relieved from hardship but so he could continue serving Christ by proclaiming the gospel (Philippians 1:19-26). Jesus exhorts his disciples to make evangelism an earnest matter of prayer. Such prayer should be frequent and fervent. Do we engage in such passionate pleading with the Lord?

Why should we engage in such prayer? If we love Jesus we will want to obey his commands. But in addition to that, Jesus gave two reasons why we should 'pray earnestly to the Lord of the harvest to send out labourers'. Firstly, because 'the harvest is plentiful' and that phrase has been generally understood as a metaphor indicating that many people are ready to hear the gospel. In other words, that many people are ripe to receive Jesus Christ as their Saviour. This interpretation seems to gain some support from our Lord's words in John chapter four, when he pointed to the Samaritans coming out from Sychar to meet him because of the testimony of the woman Jesus talked with at Jacob's well. Jesus pointed to them and said to his disciples: 'Do you not say, "There are yet four months, then comes the harvest?" Look, I tell you, lift up your eyes, and see that the fields are white for harvest. Already the one who reaps is receiving wages and gathering fruit for eternal life, so that sower and reaper may rejoice together' (John 4:35-36). What happened over the next several days appears to bear this out because, 'many more believed because of his word' (John 4:41). This indicates that many Samaritans came to saving faith in Jesus during his two-day stay in that city.

The idea that people are ripe to hear the gospel may or may not be Jesus' point in Luke chapter ten, where it is recorded that he sent out his disciples and seventy others in pairs saying, 'The harvest is plentiful, but the labourers are few. Therefore pray earnestly to the Lord of the harvest to send out labourers into his harvest' (Luke 10:2). In this case it should be noted Jesus did not promise his disciples they would meet with great success. Instead, he said, 'I am sending you out as lambs in the midst of wolves' (Luke 10:3). A few verses later, he added that those who did not receive his disciples or their message would be punished more severely in the Day of Judgment than the inhabitants of Sodom (Luke 10:10-15).

The harvest of which Christ speaks has also been understood as 'all the lost or those who are seeking after God'. But it could also be understood to refer to impending judgment on unrepentant sinners. The prophet Joel said, 'Put in the sickle, for the harvest is ripe. Go in, tread, for the winepress is full. The vats overflow, for their evil is great. Multitudes, multitudes, in the valley of decision! For the day of the LORD is near in the valley of decision' (Joel 3:13-14). In this instance, the harvest clearly has to do with God's judgment and people are pictured as facing a decision (prior to that harvest) that will seal their eternal destiny.

In the parable of the wheat and tares, Jesus spoke of two types of plants being allowed to grow together in the same field until the harvest. He then went on to say that in the time of the harvest he will instruct the reapers to gather up the tares and bind them in bundles to be burned and to gather the wheat into his barn (Matthew 13:30). Here the harvest imagery is clearly one of blessing for Christ's redeemed people but it is also just as clearly a time of judgment for those who have rejected Christ.

In the book of Revelation the apostle John described God's judgment in terms of a harvest (Revelation 14:14-19). Once again, the harvest imagery is unmistakably associated — not with people being ripe for salvation — but being ripe for God's judgment.

So, when Jesus said that the harvest is plentiful he may not have been saying people are ripe to hear the gospel and be saved, as we often think. Indeed, while that may be true occasionally in some parts of the world, the opposite is true in many other places, especially in Europe and North America where few seem interested in hearing the true gospel. So it is more likely Jesus was saying there are plentiful numbers of people who need to repent and be saved before the time of God's judgment comes.

The second reason Jesus gave for earnest prayer for harvest labourers is because the workers are few. The contrast between a plentiful harvest and few workers helps us to see the necessity for getting involved. Jesus' solution to this scarcity of workers is prayer. Interestingly, Jesus did not command his disciples to pray for the lost, although that is certainly appropriate. Rather, he instructed them to pray that the Lord of the harvest would send out workers into his harvest. It is his harvest, not ours. Therefore, he has the right to determine who will work the fields. Those who work the harvest must be God-sent, not self-appointed. They must be men and women who love God and the lost.

We are without excuse if we disobey our Saviour's command regarding such prayer. John Calvin said,

> As no man will of himself become a sincere and faithful minister of the gospel, and as none discharge in a proper manner the office of teacher but those whom the Lord raises up and endows with the gifts of His Spirit, whenever we observe a scarcity of pastors, we must raise our eyes to Him to afford the remedy. There never was greater necessity for offering this prayer than during the fearful desolation of the church which we now see every where around us.[2]

I would suggest a similar 'fearful desolation' can be found in Western society today. Many false shepherds stand in pulpits week after week. Many more sow their false seed via television and/or the Internet. False gospels are prevalent everywhere. These watered-down versions of the gospel are proclaimed for the sake of trying to attract attendees and grow churches. Surely it is a time to beseech the Lord of the harvest to send workers into his harvest. We need to get serious about asking God to raise up pastors, teachers, and evangelists who will unashamedly proclaim the whole truth of the gospel of Jesus Christ without compromise and without fear or favour. However, this is not just about getting more pastors, preachers, teachers, evangelists and church planters. This is an exhortation to all Christians to get off the couch and start fulfilling their obligations to be witnesses for Jesus.

We should start making this prayer part of our own regular prayer time. We need to get this on the agenda of the church prayer meetings and also to incorporate it into our personal devotions.

Note

1. The power and influence of social networks on the internet in disseminating the message of the gospel cannot be overestimated.
2. *Calvin's Commentaries: Vol. XVI; Commentary on the Harmony of the Evangelists, Matthew, Mark, and Luke*, p.420.

7

Developing a theology of evangelism

'... as many as were appointed to eternal life believed'
(Acts 13:48).

In Romans chapter one Paul said that the gospel is the power of God for salvation. The gospel has transformative power. It is God's way of radically changing a person's life. However, the preaching of the gospel can have negative results too. This is partly because most people do not like being told they are sinners, even though Scripture says, 'all have sinned and fall short of the glory of God' (Romans 3:23). People don't like being told God is angry with them on account of their sins, even though the Bible says, 'God is a righteous judge, and a God who feels indignation every day' (Psalm 7:11). People don't like to hear there isn't anything they can do to make themselves right with God, even though the Word of God says, 'by works of the law no human being will be justified in his sight' (Romans 3:20).

There are two distinct responses to the proclamation of the gospel in Acts chapter thirteen. Following Paul's preaching of the gospel of Jesus Christ in the city of Antioch in Pisidia (Acts

13:13-41), many of the Jews exploded with resentment and anger, while many of the Gentiles were wonderfully saved.

How does conversion take place? What does Scripture say about man's spiritual condition prior to conversion? What does the Bible say our expectations should be as we strive to be Christ's witnesses? What are we responsible for when it comes to the matter of evangelism? What are we not responsible for in evangelism? Does the Bible teach there are people who could be saved but will end up being lost? These are all important questions which need to be answered carefully and correctly because our theology will shape our approach to evangelism including our motives, the content of our message, and even the methods we use to try and bring people into Christ's kingdom.

The sovereignty of God in salvation

For many Christians, the basic principle that shapes their approach to evangelism is human sovereignty. Although this phrase is not used to describe what they believe it is nevertheless the essence of what many believe about evangelism and how conversion takes place. For example, many Christians believe that despite the impact of the Fall, every unsaved person has a spark of spiritual life inside which gives them the ability and freedom to choose equally between accepting or rejecting God's plan of salvation. But Paul explained to the Ephesians that those who have come to faith in Christ were once dead in their trespasses and sins (Ephesians 2:1, 5). There is a stark contrast here between spiritual death and spiritual life. Everybody understands that those who are dead physically cannot do anything for themselves. This is a self-evident truth. And yet, many Christians believe that those who are spiritually dead have the ability to make a choice between accepting and rejecting Christ as their Saviour, whereas the truth is that God supplies the grace to respond.

In support of this popular but false view, verses like the one found in Revelation 3:20 are quoted, where Jesus says, 'Behold, I stand at the door and knock. If anyone hears my voice and opens the door, I will come in to him and eat with him, and he with me' (Revelation 3:20). But this verse is taken out of context to support an erroneous theology. Taken in context Jesus speaks these words to a church, that is, to people who have been redeemed and who have already come to faith in Christ. It is not that those who choose to open the door will be saved and those who choose not to open the door will not be saved. All who come to faith in Christ willingly respond to the overtures of God's grace because God has quickened their spirit by his grace. It is certainly true that those who respond to the message of the gospel in repentance and faith are saved, while those who don't are not.

The attribute of sovereignty is what makes God, God. God said to Moses, 'I will be gracious to whom I will be gracious, and will show mercy on whom I will show mercy' (Exodus 33:19; Romans 9:15). Paul concluded from this: 'So then it depends not on human will or exertion, but on God, who has mercy' (Romans 9:16). The Bible teaches that only God, not man, is sovereign in salvation. Thus Jesus said, 'You did not choose me, but I chose you' (John 15:16). The apostle Paul says that God, 'chose us in him before the foundation of the world ... In love he predestined us for adoption as sons through Jesus Christ, according to the purpose of his will, to the praise of his glorious grace' (Ephesians 1:3-6).

What bearing, then, does the knowledge that God is sovereign in salvation have on us as we go about the business of trying to fulfil Christ's instruction to us to be his witnesses?

First, it tells us that the eternal destiny of men and women is not in our hands, but is rather in God's hands. To think I might be responsible for even one person missing out on heaven and going to hell is an unbearable burden. And yet, this kind of guilt trip is often used to try and motivate people to tell others about Christ. Hence, it is a great relief to know that '... as many as were appointed to eternal life believed' (Acts 13:48). None whom God has 'appointed to eternal life' are going to be lost because of my sin, my frailty, or my mistakes. With regard to evangelism this is liberating. Jesus said, 'All that the Father gives me will come to me, and whoever comes to me I will never cast out ... And this is the will of him who sent me, that I should lose nothing of all that he has given me, but raise it up on the last day' (John 6:37, 39).

There is a difference, however, between being held responsible for the eternal destiny of someone else, and being held responsible for obeying the Lord's instruction to be his witness. We will not be held accountable for the former but we will certainly have to answer for the latter. It is the moral responsibility of the Christian to obey the Lord and to seek to do his will. Indeed, obedience is one measure of our love, since Jesus once said, 'If you love me, you will keep my commandments' (John 14:15).

Second, since God is sovereign in salvation we don't have to water down the gospel to try and make it palatable to as many people as possible. We don't have to modify the message to try and get more people saved. We don't have to compromise the truth, or leave out important details, such as how offensive sin is to God, and the need for repentance. That means we can preach and teach the true gospel. We are to preach the gospel that says all people without exception are sinners (Ecclesiastes 7:20). We are to preach the gospel that says God is angry with all of us because we have sinned against him (Psalm 7:11). This is different to the popular message that 'God loves you and has a wonderful plan for your life'. Rather, it is the gospel that God's wrath abides on all of us on account of our sins (John 3:36). It is the gospel which proclaims that God has graciously provided a Saviour for sinners, whose name is Jesus (Acts 4:12). The gospel also says salvation is a free gift of God's grace (Romans 6:23). Thus salvation is not something we deserve, earn, or contribute to in the slightest degree. Thus any so-called 'gospel' that adds some human work, including baptism (as a means of regeneration), is a false gospel (Ephesians 2:8-9). The gospel also says no one is a Christian unless they have repented of their sins and professed faith in Jesus Christ (Acts 20:21), both of which God graciously enables us to do (John 15:5).

The gospel also says those who are saved by God's grace will give evidence of it by their good works (Ephesians 2:10). The gospel produces changed lives which are reoriented toward God (Ephesians 4:22-24).

Most unsaved people want to hear what nice people they are or what nice people they can become if they just make a few minor adjustments. Most unsaved people want a list of things they can do to improve their lives or, better yet, they want hear what God intends to do to make their life better. Most unsaved people (and sadly many Christians too) do not want sound doctrine. They want to hear things that are pleasing to them (2 Timothy 4:3). Many people want their conscience eased, and their egos soothed. Most unsaved people want to be reassured everything is okay. But that is not what they hear when the true gospel is preached and that is why so many find it deeply offensive. And because people find the gospel offensive some 'preachers' want to dilute it. But the gospel should not be sugar-coated to make it more palatable. Preached in the anointed power of the Holy Spirit it is a potent force which brings conviction of sin and can lead to repentance and faith in Christ as Saviour and Lord.

The church can be very popular if it does not preach the gospel. It can be popular if it avoids mentioning sin, judgment, hell etc. If the church focuses only on people's felt needs and gives people feel-good messages it will be popular. If the church is a community centre that just engages in social projects and neglects to preach the true gospel then many people will embrace it. But however fervently committed people are to such projects they are not saved unless, and until, they repent of their sins and turn to Christ for salvation.

Though many unsaved people will find the gospel offensive, we should not give them a justifiable reason to find us offensive. On the contrary, the Bible says we are not to put obstacles in anyone's way (2 Corinthians 6:3).

We need to be reminded of what our own spiritual condition was before we were saved. We need to see the true spiritual condition of people in the world. We cannot be effective witnesses for Christ unless we have a biblically informed spiritual perspective on this matter. Neither can we be effective witnesses by relying solely on our abilities and talents. We depend on the enabling grace of God through the empowering of the Holy Spirit. Jesus once told his disciples, 'apart from me you can do nothing' (John 15:5).

What is the spiritual condition of the people with whom we are dealing? What is the spiritual condition of those to whom we are trying to explain the gospel? What is the spiritual condition of the people with whom we are trying to build relationships, in hope of being able to tell them about Jesus Christ? The Bible gives us numerous pictures that describe the people with whom we are dealing. These pictures also remind us of what we were like before we repented of our sins and professed faith in Christ. Romans chapter five gives us such a picture. There we are presented with the truth that we were weak and helpless sinners and enemies of God (Romans 5:6, 8, 10).

Who are we dealing with as we go about trying to be witnesses for Jesus? According to Romans chapter five, we are dealing with people who are utterly helpless to save themselves, sinners by nature as well as behaviour, and enemies of God, in part because they are constantly resisting his will and breaking his commands. The Bible clearly teaches that unredeemed people are enslaved to sin (John 8:34; Romans 6:6) and that outside of Christ people are dead in their trespasses and sins (Ephesians 2:1). Although physical death is one consequence of sin, the deadness spoken of in Ephesians is spiritual in nature. Spiritual death is a very real and far more serious condition than many people realize. Just as physical death separates us from those we know and love, so spiritual death separates us from God (Isaiah 59:2). It separates us from his friendship and love and ultimately, for those who do not repent and profess faith in Christ, they will be separated from his presence in heaven (Luke 16:26).

Many people like to believe that the gulf between the living and the dead can be bridged. There are books and movies that promote this sentimental and spiritually untrue idea. The living may enjoy pleasant memories of the dead and remain close to their deceased loved ones in their affections; but physical death puts an end to our relationships. Once a person dies, communication with them is no longer possible. That chasm of separation brought about by death and the ensuing times of grief and loneliness make this reality very clear. The heartache of the bereaved shows just how real and how serious death is. Paul uses this image to convey the reality and seriousness of spiritual death. The spiritually dead do not have any kind of positive relationship with the living God (Psalm 42:2). Unconfessed and therefore unforgiven sin separates people from God. In fact there is a negative relationship between the unredeemed and God. Their relationship with God is one of aversion rather than affection, hostility rather than friendship and hatred rather than love. There are bumper stickers that say 'God loves you' but I have never seen one that proclaims 'God hates you'. I am not commending either of these truncated statements as abridged versions of the gospel.

No person can be spiritually alive and spiritually dead at the same time, any more than light and darkness can co-exist in the same physical space (2 Corinthians 6:14). There can be one or the other but there cannot be both.

The separation that characterizes spiritual death is illustrated in Genesis chapter three, where one of the first things Adam and Eve did after they sinned against God was try and hide themselves from him (Genesis 3:8), even though prior to that moment they had enjoyed a close, intimate relationship with him. God had instructed them not to eat from the tree of the knowledge of good and evil, warning that if they did so they would surely die (Genesis 2:17). They did not die physically until many years later but spiritual death was instantaneous and resulted in separation from God. This idea of spiritual death is vividly conveyed in the words of the prophet Isaiah: 'but your iniquities have made a separation between you and your God, and your sins have hidden his face from you so that he does not hear' (Isaiah 59:2). This is the true spiritual condition of every unsaved person. Because they are dead they have neither the ability nor the desire to change. People in this condition do not accept the things of the Spirit of God because they are foolishness to them. They cannot understand them, because such things are spiritually apprehended (1 Corinthians 2:14).

As we talk with our friends and neighbours and co-workers about Christ, we need to remember we are dealing with people who, like Nicodemus (John 3:9-10), do not understand what we are talking about, despite whatever intellectual capacity or level of education they may have. We have to remember we are dealing with people who are spiritually dead. That means they are incapable of responding. They are not people who still have a few spiritual reflexes left, if we can just find them. We are dealing with people who need to be spiritually resurrected. This is what being 'born again' really means (John 3:3-8). They are not people who simply need to be awakened from a coma. They need to be regenerated.

Regeneration may be illustrated by considering what happened to Lazarus when Jesus raised him from the dead. The Lord did not reawaken Lazarus from a state of unconsciousness. Scripture tells us Lazarus had been in the tomb four days by the time Jesus arrived at Bethany (John 11:17). The effect of this delay ensured that everyone knew Lazarus was really and truly dead and not merely in a state of unconsciousness. When Jesus instructed that the stone covering the tomb be removed Martha protested, saying, 'Lord, by this time there will be an odour, for he has been dead four days' (John 11:39). Once the stone was removed, Jesus offered a brief prayer (John 11:41-42) then cried out with a loud voice: 'Lazarus, come forth' (John 11:43) and Lazarus emerged from his grave, alive (John 11:44). How could a man who had been dead four days respond to Christ's command? Jesus had (and still has) supernatural authority over death. Lazarus was physiologically regenerated.

The same kind of thing needs to happen spiritually to those who are dead in their trespasses and sins. Before those we are witnessing to can respond in repentance and faith, they must be regenerated by the Holy Spirit. They have to be called forth by the voice of Almighty God. This is what Jesus really meant when he said to Nicodemus: 'Truly, truly, I say to you, unless one is born again he cannot see the kingdom of God' (John 3:3). Before lost people can respond to the message of the gospel they need to have a supernatural heart-transplant. They need to have their heart of stone removed and replaced with a heart of flesh, that is, a dead heart replaced with a living one which is receptive to and responsive to the voice of God (Ezekiel 36:26). They need to have their deaf ears divinely unstopped and their blind eyes miraculously opened (Isaiah 35:5). Only then will they be able to understand the message of salvation and see their need for a Saviour. Only then will they want to respond to our witness by repenting of their sin and professing faith in Jesus Christ and only then will they be able to actually do it.

We cannot impart spiritual life to people who are spiritually dead. That is something God alone can do. When we were dead in our trespasses and sins it was God who made us alive in Christ and our salvation was entirely an act of his grace (Ephesians 2:5). God performed no less a miracle in giving us spiritual life than Jesus did in giving new life to Lazarus.

What affect will this have on our evangelistic efforts? We should not be surprised when they do not understand, nor should we become too discouraged when the people we have built a relationship with don't respond positively to the gospel. We can be saddened by this but we should not be surprised. We also need to realize that their rejection of our witness has nothing to do with our approach, or our method, or our inability to understand postmodern culture. That does not mean we shouldn't be concerned about these things. It simply means these things are not the crux of the problem. We do not have the power, in and of ourselves, to change that. Their rejection of the gospel is not our fault. This means we do not have to feel guilty every time our witness fails to produce the desired results. There are plenty of things in life we might legitimately feel guilty about but this is not one of them. We might as well beat ourselves up over not being able to raise people from the dead. We must accept that we will not be able to win over every person we talk to about Christ. That means all the credit for any success we do have belongs to the Lord. He alone deserves the praise for any people who come to Christ through our efforts.

The fact that God alone gives life to those who are spiritually dead also means all our witnessing, all our evangelism training, all our relationship building needs to be preceded and accompanied by fervent prayer — prayer which pleads that God would be merciful to the people we are witnessing to. We should pray that God would regenerate the spiritually dead so they can hear and understand and respond to the message of the gospel. We should pray that God would be pleased to use us to draw some to Christ in repentance and faith.

Scripture speaks of those whom God has chosen (2 Peter 1:20-21) from among all the sinners on earth to be God's special possession (1 Peter 2:9). Those adopted into the family of Christ are not chosen because there was anything in them that made them worthy or deserving but simply because God chose to love them unconditionally (Deuteronomy 7:7). Furthermore God imparts to the elect both the desire and ability to repent of their sins and profess faith in Jesus Christ (Ephesians 2:8-9). Because we do not know whom God has chosen we cannot be selective about whom we will witness to. Pray, therefore, that God will lead us to those he has chosen.

May we have the willingness that Paul had (2 Timothy 2:8-10) and, more importantly, Jesus had (Philippians 2:5-8) to endure whatever we must for the sake of the gospel. Immediately prior to Jesus ascending to heaven he entrusted his disciples with the mission of being witnesses for him. This mandate is not just for the eleven men who were with Jesus that day (Acts 1:1-6). It is not just for the one-hundred-and-twenty men and women who later gathered together in an upper room to devote themselves to prayer (Acts 1:13-15). It was not just for those who were present on the Day of Pentecost (Acts 2:1-4). This mandate is for every person who has repented of their sins and professed faith in Jesus Christ as Saviour and Lord. It is a mandate for all believers.

Every Christian has the Holy Spirit dwelling within (Romans 8:14-16; 2 Corinthians 1:21-22). That means there is no such thing as a Christian from whom God the Father has withheld the power to be one of Christ's witnesses. The issue then is about learning to be what we already are in Christ (Ephesians 5:7-10). Hence, the only question is, what kind of witness will we be?

We do not have to worry if our witness is not exactly like someone else's because God has made us all different, and uniquely gifted us (Matthew 25:14-15; 1 Corinthians 12:4-11). Will we hide our light under a basket or will we set it on a stand where it can give off as much illumination as possible (Matthew 5:15)?

Our theology will make a significant difference to our motivation and methods. Our whole approach will be governed by our theological understanding. If we believe God has predestined a certain number of people to eternal life, and that these people are going to be saved whether we do anything or not, then we may not be motivated to tell others about Christ, or even support the efforts of those who are trying to do so.[1]

On the other hand, if we believe the number of people who end up in heaven depends on how hard we work then we are going to use any and every means possible (be they biblical or borrowed from the world) to get people to make a profession of faith in Christ.[2]

God's sovereignty over salvation means the eternal destiny of men and women is in his hands, not ours. As we seek to be Christ's witnesses we are to go into the entire world and preach the gospel to all (Mark 16:15). We are to go and make disciples of all the nations (Matthew 28:19). We are to be Christ's witnesses not only in Jerusalem, Judea and Samaria but also in the remotest parts of the earth (Acts 1:8).

The book of Revelation gives us a glimpse of the end result of the redemptive work of Christ. There we are told that Jesus has purchased souls (with his blood) from every tribe and tongue and people and nation (Revelation 5:9). That book reveals the fact that a time is approaching when a great multitude that nobody can count from every nation, and all the tribes and peoples and tongues of this world will stand before God's throne and worship him (Revelation 7:9-10). Thus we are not searching for anyone in particular. We are simply looking for opportunities to share the gospel with anybody who will listen. We are searching for anyone who will talk with us about spiritual matters, come to a home Bible study or accept our invitation to attend church. But in another sense we are searching for those whom 'God chose ... to be saved, through sanctification by the Spirit and belief in the truth' (2 Thessalonians 2:13). As we do not know who these people are, we witness to all without reservation.

Again, since we do not know who God's chosen people are and as they don't have a 'C' (for 'Chosen') tattooed on their foreheads we are to witness to all who are willing to listen. Like the sower Jesus spoke of in Matthew chapter thirteen, we are to scatter the seed of the gospel everywhere we can, even though we know that only some of it will fall on good ground (Matthew 13:3-8). Like the fisherman Jesus spoke of in that same chapter, we are to cast as wide a net as possible (Matthew 13:47-50).

A brief lesson in church history

Over four hundred years ago, in 1610, the followers of a Dutch seminary professor named James Arminius, drew up five articles of faith based on their late mentor's teaching. These men, who came to be known as 'Arminians', presented their five doctrinal positions to the Church of Holland in the form of a 'Remonstrance' (or 'protest'), in hope of getting the church to change its official Catechism and Confession of Faith to conform to their theological views.

These five articles of faith may be summarized as follows. First, God elects or rejects people on the basis of foreseen faith or unbelief. Second, that Christ died for everybody, although only believers will be saved. Third, that man is so depraved that divine grace is necessary for faith or any good deed. Fourth, the grace God offers for such matters can be resisted or rejected. Fifth, that it is possible for a truly saved believer to lose his faith, and therefore lose his salvation.

This theology is based on two presuppositions, namely that God's sovereignty is incompatible with man's freedom and human responsibility and that man's ability limits his obligations. Arminius and his followers drew two wrong conclusions from these philosophical principles. First, since the Bible regards faith as a free and responsible act (which is true), it cannot be caused by God (which is mistaken) — rather, the faith required for salvation is something man exercises independently of God (another wrong conclusion). Second, since the Bible regards faith as obligatory on the part of all who hear the gospel (which is true) the ability to believe must be universal. This too is a wrong conclusion.

Arminius and his followers errantly reasoned that God's command to all men to believe the gospel in order to be saved means the ability to believe must be inherently present in all men otherwise God is being unfair or unreasonable.

In light of these conclusions, the Arminians said Scripture must be interpreted as teaching the following positions. First, man is never so completely corrupted by sin that he cannot believe the gospel when it is put before him. Second, man is never so completely controlled by God that he cannot reject the gospel. Third, God's election of those who shall be saved is prompted by his foreseeing they will believe of their own accord (i.e. with little or no direct influence from God). Fourth, Christ's death did not guarantee the salvation of anyone, because it did not secure the gift of faith for anyone (indeed, there is no such gift). What Christ's death did was create the possibility of salvation for everyone (albeit only on the condition they believe). Fifth, it rests with believers to keep themselves in a state of grace by keeping up their faith. Otherwise they will fall away and be lost.

These interpretations differed significantly from what was considered to be the orthodox view of Scripture at that point in church history. Arminianism made man's salvation depend ultimately on man himself. Saving faith came to be considered (in this theological framework) as man's own work rather than God's work of grace.

In 1618, the Church of Holland called a synod for the purpose of examining the views of Arminianism in the light of Scripture. The synod met 154 times in the city of Dort over a six-month period (from 13 November 1618 until 9 May 1619). Moreover, among its 102 official delegates were 27 representatives from countries other than Holland — like Germany, Switzerland and England.

This synod scrutinized the five points presented by the remonstrants and compared the teaching advanced in them with the testimony of Scripture. Failing to reconcile that teaching with the Scripture (which they had declared beforehand could alone be accepted by them as the ultimate rule of doctrine and faith) they unanimously rejected all five points.

The synod felt, however, that a mere rejection was not sufficient. They felt obliged to set forth the true teaching of God's Word in relation to those matters which had been called into question. Because John Calvin (who had died some fifty years earlier, in 1564) had done so much to explain and defend these views, the response of the Synod (*The Canons of Dort*) became known historically as 'the five points of Calvinism'. These five points are sometimes summarized by the acrostic **TULIP**, **T**otal Depravity, **U**nconditional Election, **L**imited Atonement, **I**rresistible Grace and the **P**erseverance of the Saints.

The Synod of Dort was an orthodox gathering of church leaders, not some group on the theological fringe. Many people today find it strange that such an important church body would have rejected the five articles advanced by the followers of James Arminius, especially since these same doctrines are probably held by a majority of people in the contemporary church. Indeed, many people in the contemporary church are genuinely surprised to learn that there is another view. This 'other view' not only has the weight of church history behind it but even more importantly it has the weight of Scripture in its favour.

It is a view that says that salvation is a work of God's grace from beginning to end. It upholds the scriptural truth that in no sense does a sinner save himself or contribute to his salvation. Adam's fall totally ruined the human race. Thus all men are by virtue of their fallen nature, spiritually dead and their wills enslaved to sin and Satan. Thus the ability to believe the gospel is a gift from God, given to those whom he has chosen to be the objects of his unmerited favour. And that once a sinner has been saved he or she can never lose their salvation, because God has graciously promised to preserve them.

All those whom Jesus died to save will eventually believe and be saved; while all those for whom he did not die will not believe, and therefore not be saved. Jesus said that he came to 'give his life a ransom for many' (Mark 10:45). He never said he would give his life a ransom for all. What he came to do was to die for all those the Father gave him before the world was created. Jesus did exactly what he came to do. Thus Paul could tell Timothy: 'Therefore I endure everything for the sake of the elect, that they also may obtain the salvation that is in Christ Jesus with eternal glory' (2 Timothy 2:10).

This may sound heretical and offensive to many, especially if they have been going to church for a number of years and are suddenly confronted with it for the first time. This doctrine more than any other has a direct practical bearing on the way we go about presenting the gospel to those with whom we are trying to build a relationship.

Understanding that a person's salvation is God's choice (made before the foundation of the world) is not an excuse for complacency about sharing the message of the gospel but it does remove the tyranny of the idea that salvation depends on our ability to persuade and lead people to making a decision.

This is a pertinent matter that needs to be addressed if the truth is to be better understood in relation to evangelism. Much that is published today about evangelism is driven by an Arminian understanding of the importance and urgency of human responsibility in evangelism. What is needed, however, is a more balanced and biblical perspective in the theology of mission.

Many scriptures attest that salvation is God's choice (e.g. Romans 8:29-30; Ephesians 1:4-6, 11). Furthermore, Scripture tells us when that choice was made, 'he chose us in him before the foundation of the world' (Ephesians 1:4).

The doctrine of predestination is clearly taught in Scripture. Those who would seek to deny it are not being faithful exegetes of these texts. However, in an effort to dilute this teaching (which is, in essence, an attempt to deny it) many have sought to redefine the term 'predestination'. They equate predestination with God's foreknowledge. This is a serious distortion. Although it is a notion that has found widespread acceptance it is utterly odious to God. Calvin says, 'Men do not gain the favour of God by their free-will, but are chosen by his goodness alone before they were born'.

Many people who countenance the idea of an omniscient God who foresees how people will respond to the gospel and predestines to eternal life those whom he foresees responding in faith are merely ignorant of scriptural truth. W. R. Godfrey says:

> *The contemporary evangelical church has become largely Arminian, often as a result of anti-doctrinal bias rather than careful theological reflection. The historic Augustinian doctrine of predestination remains biblically and theologically compelling.*[3]

But there are also intellectual advocates of this view, who encourage others to consider the Augustinian / Calvinistic view as invalid. I would not want to question their integrity but I do attribute such belief to poor judgment.

The key verses in the Arminian armoury are 2 Thessalonians 2:13 and Romans 8:29-30. They seem to support their position regarding foreknowledge. However, God's foreknowledge does not merely mean knowledge in advance of some event happening (prescience). God's foreknowledge is knowledge based upon a plan. As such it means not just to know beforehand but to love beforehand (fore-love).

In Romans 9:14 Paul asks the question: 'Is God unjust?' The resounding answer exclaimed by the apostle is 'Not at all!' If unconditional election is not being taught in Romans chapter nine, why raise and answer this question? Obviously Paul is anticipating objections to this teaching and addresses the issue. He is addressing a charge that presupposes he will be understood as teaching unconditional election. If Paul were teaching universal election or divine election without that unconditional element, nobody would raise a question about God's fairness. The issue of the injustice of God never arises in the Arminian theory because it is seen as a judicious foreordination. Paul does not equivocate on the issue and he does not present a rational explanation to pacify doubters. He simply says, 'Not at all!' Don't say it and don't think it because it is not true.

Verse sixteen directly addresses the Arminian issue. It does not, therefore, depend on man's desire or effort, but on God's mercy. Man is free to make choices but that freedom is limited by his fallen nature. He has only his perverse rational powers to guide him to follow his depraved inclinations.

Socinus (1539–1604), the forerunner of Unitarianism, who was deemed to be a heretic by the Christian church, translated Scripture in a manner that suited his theories. Acts 13:38 says, 'All who were appointed for eternal life believed,' but he put it in the reverse order: 'All who believed were appointed for eternal life'. This distortion of Scripture is popular today.

Arminianism is a man-centred theory whereas Calvinism is a God-centred perspective. Election is not merely a ratification of man's decision. As John Owen put it: 'Christ did not die for any upon condition, if they believe; but he died for all God's elect, that they should believe.' What is truly amazing in election is not that God chose only some but that he chose any!

Since the fall of Adam man in his lost and sinful condition is at enmity with God. His fallen and rebellious nature is so corrupted that he has neither the desire nor the inclination to seek after God. Salvation, therefore, must, of necessity, come from God's gracious initiative. Calvin said, 'God ... wrote the names of his children in the Book of life before the creation of the world; but he enrolls them in the catalogue of his saints only when, having regenerated them by the spirit of adoption, he impresses his own mark upon them.'

The election of a soul to salvation does not depend on any virtue in the individual. A person is elected to salvation in accordance with God's sovereign purpose by his eternal and inscrutable decree. It is based on the goodwill and pleasure of God alone. As to when God's choice was settled, we uphold Calvin's view that, 'The election of God is anterior to Adam's fall.'

The reason why some are rescued while others are passed over is a mystery to the rational mind that seems to breach our understanding of the notion of justice. To some, God may appear to be capricious and even callous. But there is nothing whimsical or arbitrary in God's choice. Election is not the random and indifferent action of a despotic God. Rather it magnifies his grace. Grace has often been presented as God's unmerited favour to the undeserving but that is a definition that fails to explain fully the true nature of grace because grace is, rather, God's unmerited favour, not to the undeserving, but to the hell-deserving! The reprobate, therefore, receive what they deserve and the seriousness of sin is stressed in their eternal punishment.

It is right to be unequivocal and unashamed of this glorious truth as the authentic teaching of Scripture, but it is ugly where there is a haughty spirit when humility would be more appropriate. The keynote for a befitting attitude to the profundity of predestination may well be taken from Paul's great doxological statement: 'Oh, the depth of the riches and wisdom and knowledge of God! How unsearchable are his judgements and how inscrutable his ways! "For who has known the mind of the Lord...?"' (Romans 11:33-34). However, we must assert this truth in love, not only to affirm our own faith but also to establish others in a truly biblical understanding of election. Spurgeon said that some medicine is better swallowed than chewed: 'In the same way there are some things in the Word of God which are undoubtedly true which must be swallowed at once by an effort of faith, and must not be chewed by perpetual questioning.'

Rightly grasped, the doctrine of unconditional election should be a stimulus to evangelism. Understanding election ought to inspire rather than inhibit evangelism. We have a duty to desire all men to be saved and this attitude will inform and motivate our evangelism. In praying for all to be saved and preaching to all that they must be saved we leave their election to God's eternal and inscrutable discretion. We must bear in mind that God has appointed preaching and evangelism as the means by which he will accomplish his saving purposes. Our understanding of election should not restrict our preaching. This is a crucial matter and it seems strange that an appreciation of this truth can have the effect of gagging gospel preaching.

Iain Murray addresses this issue: 'While Reformed Confessions may begin with statements on the doctrine of God and divine decrees, that is not where preachers and teachers need to begin in addressing men about salvation'.[4] He points out that in the apostolic and evangelistic preaching of Acts no mention is made of the doctrine of election but that the epistles emphasize this truth. He then says, 'In accordance with this approach, Calvin, in the later editions of his *Institutes*, moved his treatment of election to follow teaching on justification. He recognized that Scripture generally introduces the doctrine of election to show believers the security and certainty of their salvation...'[5]

Evangelism should be motivated primarily by a concern for the glory of God and obedience to Christ's commission (Matthew 28:19). It ought to be a spontaneous outworking of our gratitude for God's grace. It must be inspired by a concern for the eternal destiny of souls.

Nevertheless there is no time to waste. We should not procrastinate by putting off getting actively involved in fulfilling Christ's mandate to be his witnesses. Most believers will never be called to preach the gospel. Many will find the confrontational method of evangelism distasteful and difficult, but all of us can get involved in building relationships with non-Christians. We can do that, initially, without worrying about 'sharing the gospel', or saying something 'spiritual', or inviting people to church. Obviously, if a door of opportunity presents itself, we should take advantage of it. If we have been gifted in the area of proclamation evangelism or confrontational evangelism then we should do what we have been gifted to do. But for most Christians the goal right now is much simpler. Let us just look for opportunities to build relationships with some non-Christians. That ought not to be a terrifying prospect for any individual unless they have social and psychological problems, in which case they need help. The vast majority of Christians will not have a spiritual problem with such an approach to being witnesses for Jesus.

Notes

1. This is the inappropriate response of some hyper-Calvinists.
2. This is the inappropriate response of some Arminians.
3. Godfrey, W. R. 'Predestination', *New Dictionary of Theology,* p.530.
4. *Spurgeon v Hyper-Calvinism: The Battle for Gospel Preaching,* Banner of Truth, 1995, p.152.
5. Op. cit.

8
Practical advice

'... let your light shine before others, so that they may see your good works and give glory to your Father who is in heaven'
(Matthew 5:16).

Jesus socialized with tax collectors and other sinners so often the self-righteous began referring to him disparagingly as 'a friend of tax collectors and sinners' (Matthew 11:19). Whereas they would cross the street to avoid passing a known sinner on the roadside, Jesus would go to the homes of 'sinners' and eat meals with them! When we talk about Jesus eating with sinners we need to remember we were once in that category ourselves and that had he not humbled himself to befriend us we would still be lost in our sins. Indeed we are sinners but now we are saved sinners, sanctified by grace.

Jesus did not walk up to people he met for the first time and say, 'Hi, I'm God's Messiah and I'd like to tell you why you need to believe in me to be saved.' Scripture indicates Jesus spent time building friendships with people. This explains why the scribes and Pharisees were so critical of him for socializing with sinners.

But many Christians find the simple proposition of trying to build positive relationships with non-believers difficult, if not actually frightening. What we need, therefore, is some practical suggestions about how to make friends with non-Christians.

Not every non-believing neighbour, acquaintance or co-worker is going to want to be our friend. We should remain cordial and look for those who are willing to respond to our overtures of friendship. All our efforts to build relationships with non-believers need to be under-girded by prayer. Evangelism is a process that requires planting, watering and weeding before we can even think about a harvest.

So Jesus had a reputation for spending time with the unconverted. By contrast, many Christians today spend most of their time with the converted. Many don't have any genuine friendships with non-believers, despite the fact that they interact with them every day at work, at school and so on.

Scott Morton tells of the time he taught a Sunday school class on evangelism to a group of young married couples. These were bright people with promising careers who were socially in tune. After spending several weeks laying the biblical groundwork, he passed out index cards and gave the following assignment: 'Think of the non-believers in your world — at work, in your neighbourhood, at the health club, and so on. List the names of those you could invite to your home for a meal on a Friday or Saturday night in the next few weeks. Your goal is not to spring the gospel on them, but to just enjoy a nice evening together.'[1]

Morton says there was a long silence. Class members stared at him then at their index cards and finally off into the air. Eventually, a few began doodling on their card as if hoping a name or two might magically appear from the end of their pen. After a while, one class member spoke up and said, 'Scott, we have non-Christian acquaintances, but we don't have non-Christian friends and especially none we want to invite into our homes.' They were nervous about inviting these people to their homes in case they took the Lord's name in vain and in case they wanted to drink alcohol or smoke!

With regard to alcohol the Bible teaches moderation not abstinence. It is true to say that whereas drunkenness is a sin drinking alcohol is not. Even though smoking tobacco, drinking alcohol and dancing are not inherently sinful activities there are certainly health issues and addiction issues and potential moral hazards associated with these things. Christians in different cultures have different attitudes to this issue. Drinking alcohol is forbidden in some denominations. Many church constitutions and codes of practice for church members (as well as faculty and students of theological seminaries, Bible colleges and Christian universities) do not allow the consumption of alcohol. Whether a Christian drinks alcohol or not is not the critical issue in relation to evangelism. One can abstain from alcohol and still maintain friendship with non-Christians who consume alcohol. One does not have to compromise any moral principle when seeking to relate to non-Christians. Many non-Christians do not drink alcohol.

One by one other members of Morton's class spoke up, expressing similar reticence and reluctance to engage any of the non-believers they knew in genuine friendship. They were all more comfortable entertaining Christian friends, hiring Christian plumbers, taking their car to Christian mechanics, and patronizing Christian restaurants, all of which reinforces the notion that for many Christians associating with Christians is the norm, while choosing to spend free time with non-Christians (like Jesus did) is highly unusual. It is shocking that many Christians have a holier-than-thou attitude to non-Christians and have come to think of the church as a club for the holy rather than an association of sinners redeemed by God's grace.

Many Christians are content to live in their private bubbles but if we are going to be Christ's witnesses we need to break out of our insulated, sanitized world and start moving into the lives of unbelievers. Sadly, many Christians have become institutionalized in the church. This sort of thing happens to long-term prisoners so that they come to a point in their lives where the thought of freedom frightens them. They would prefer to stay in prison (where they have friends and have become familiar with the rules and code of conduct) than be released into the community. We need to stop thinking exclusively in terms of sacred space (church) and start thinking more in terms of shared space (cafés etc.). This is often referred to in contemporary missional writing as the 'third place'. We must be intentional in this process because it is unlikely to happen otherwise.

We should make a list of several non-believers to pray for. We should ask God to give us opportunities to get to know them. The Christian must take the initiative in this regard by purposefully and consistently extending invitations to non-believers to spend some time together, socially. It is preferable to not share the gospel initially on such occasions. If we spring the 'hidden agenda' on these occasions it will most likely offend and alienate. If we do that then we need not be surprised if they decline our next invitation for a 'fun evening' out. But we should not hide our faith. We should share all aspects of our lives because that is what friends do. Building a trusting relationship with non-believers takes time. Ordinarily, this is not something we can do in a single encounter or conversation.

There may be those salesmen-like personalities who can do that but most of us need more time.

Speaking of salesmen, what is your own reaction when someone comes to your door uninvited, or, as happens more often today, when a stranger calls you on the phone wanting to sell you something? Are you happy he called? Are you interested in listening to what he has to say? I suspect that you are probably not interested. On the contrary, you are more likely to have an almost automatic resistance to anything he tells you, even if he is right. But, if a friend comes by and gives you a glowing report about the very same product, your reaction is likely to be different. In that scenario you are probably going to be much more positive and receptive, even if you don't choose to buy the product.

Like it or not, many non-believers have a similar gut reaction to our attempts to tell them about Christ if we have not built some level of trust or credibility with them. But to do that takes time and it is likely to offend the religious Pharisees of our day.

In our efforts to evangelize we frequently fail to take enough time to build credibility with non-believers. We are sometimes not lacking in boldness but our tactfulness is questionable.

So how do we build credibility with non-believers? We do it by being ourselves and living a consistent Christian life. We don't hide the fact we are Christians but we don't flaunt it either. Let us, therefore, ensure that our behaviour is admirable and noble and that we do not bring the gospel into disrepute. As others observe us (and we do live in a watching world) they will be drawn to wonder what it is that makes us different. We should not be pushy propagandists for God. Rather, we should lead quiet and gentle lives so that our light shines in this dark world

(1 Peter 2:12; 1 Thessalonians 4:11-12; Matthew 5:16). If we ever want to tell our non-Christian friends about Christ, and have them listen with some degree of interest, we had better lay the groundwork beforehand so our testimony has some credibility. We don't need to be perfect, but we do need to be genuine.

So how do we go about building relationships with non-believers? I think we do it the same way we build a friendship with anyone else, i.e. we have to get to know them — and to do that we have to spend time with them. So here are a few practical suggestions.

Be friendly and be a good listener. You will be amazed at how much you can learn about your non-believing acquaintances if you concentrate on listening to what they say — whether they're talking to you or someone else. We should be quick to hear and slow to speak (James 1:19). Some reflective listening which involves summarizing both the content and emotions of what has been said is a very positive way of engaging people. This is not manipulative, it is just a good listening skill and such skills can be learned and refined with practice.

Discover what your non-believing acquaintances' interests are, and talk about those. For example, does your neighbour like to fish or does he like to work with wood? Knowing what his interests are provides us with a ready bridge to conversations that help the relationship grow, regardless of whether they are our interests or not.

Along these same lines we need to try and cultivate some common interests and build a reservoir of shared experiences. The list of possible interests is almost endless (sport, music, movies, hiking, concerts, gardening, reading, playing chess or cards, cooking, crafts, eating out, etc.). The idea is to discover potential points of contact and then use them as relational building blocks. The purpose is to use our common interests to build credibility with non-believers so that when the opportunity presents itself we can invite them to church, or to a Bible study or share Christ with them ourselves and do it as someone who is their friend, rather than someone who only seems to be interested in clinching a deal.

Most books on evangelism have been written by gifted evangelists. We can be spurred on by their exhortations and inspired by their stories but left a little frustrated by our own comparative inadequacies. After a while we become immune to exhortations from the pulpit to evangelize. We are impervious to appeals to get involved and feel that this is just not our thing. In this state of fatigue or saturation we justify our position by telling ourselves that evangelism is for evangelists, pastors and professionals who are gifted, trained and enthusiastic about it. That is partly true because evangelism is a special gift. But every Christian is called to be a witness!

Many Christians feel intensely guilty for not having tried to evangelize the butcher, the baker, their neighbour or the person trapped between them and the window on the aeroplane. They try to put every thought of 'sharing Christ' out of mind so they can have some semblance of peace. So what is the solution? Is it to confess the sin of fear, and repent for past failures to be Christ's witnesses? No doubt some of that is needed. Is the solution to take a formal evangelism training course? That might help. Is the solution to convince ourselves that since we don't have the gift of evangelism, Christ's command to be his witness does not apply to us?

The solution is not to find a way to weasel out of our responsibility to be Christ's witnesses but to find a way to fulfil that responsibility in keeping with how God has made us. In other words, the solution is not necessarily to imitate what someone else is doing, although sometimes that can be helpful. Rather, we need to find a way that fits the personality God has given us, and that makes use of the gifts with which the Holy Spirit has equipped us.

For many the solution is not to learn various techniques for witnessing to strangers and casual acquaintances. Rather, the solution is to learn how to build relationships with non-believers, so when the time comes we can share Christ with them as their friend — i.e. as someone they know cares about them, rather than a person who only seems interested in 'making a sale' or who is motivated more by a sense of guilt rather than genuine love or compassion.

There may be occasions when a condensed presentation of the gospel is needed, say, for example, if somebody is on their death-bed. In such circumstances we may not have time to share more than the barest essentials. Or if witnessing to a stranger we may never see again, we probably will not have time to go through an elaborate gospel presentation. Hence we need to be able to convey God's plan of salvation as succinctly as possible. There may be a time and place for such an approach but that is not ideal. In reality most Christians will never find themselves in situations where they are called upon to witness to someone on their death-bed. As for witnessing to strangers, I believe we need to get away from this kind of mentality. It is certainly true that people have been saved by using these methods but for most Christians the more natural way of being witnesses for Jesus is to follow our Saviour's example of building relationships with non-Christians. The only way to build friendships with non-believers is to intentionally spend time with them — a rather obvious point but one that needs to be made nevertheless.

Practical advice

People are engaged by personal stories, if they are an organic part of a conversation (not an intrusive monologue). So rather than trying to give the Christian worldview, which in this postmodern world is just another discredited 'meta-narrative' (which means 'big story'), it would be preferable to share your own 'petit-narrative' ('small story'). In postmodern culture the 'petit-narrative' is acceptable. Why not practise giving your testimony in three minutes and be observant and respectful about the rules of engagement? If the person asks questions about your conversion experience then it is acceptable to continue to share more information. If the person does not respond then the matter is closed and it is offensive to continue. If the person changes the subject then talk about the subject he has raised and hope and pray that he will feel comfortable enough to return to a discussion about the gospel once he realizes you are 'normal' and not just some automated zealot programmed with Bible verses as a substitute for conversation.

We should certainly avoid putting ourselves in situations where unbelievers exert harmful influence or control over our lives. Ideally, it is preferable to build relationships with non-believers and to take the time to develop a level of trust and credibility with them before initiating any kind of spiritual conversation. This usually takes time, effort, and a certain amount of personal sacrifice. It has already been suggested that the Christian needs to learn to be a good listener. When we speak it should not be like an interrogation, rather we should ask non-threatening questions to discover what our non-believing friend's interests are so that we can talk about those things rather than talking about ourselves most of the time.

If we invite non-believers into our homes we are increasing our chances of developing more meaningful relationships with them. Sharing a meal with others is a very good way of developing friendship. It is probably a good idea to have a reason for inviting them. If your friend is interested in wood-turning and you have a lathe and this is your hobby it makes sense to ask him around to see your handiwork or help you with a few tips and to share a bite to eat. It is better to avoid something too elaborate and contrived. Remember, the goal is to build a friendship not to torpedo the relationship before it even has a chance to develop.

What if our non-believing guests bring habits we consider 'un-Christian' into our home? Why should we be surprised when non-Christians behave like non-Christians? It is absurd for us to expect them to behave like something they are not. We should, therefore, not give the impression (by our words or facial expressions) that any future relationship we might have with them depends on their doing so. I seriously doubt that Jesus expected the sinners he ate with to behave like he did. His friendship was not contingent on their conformity to proper moral standards.

Having said that, however, how should we handle some of the 'uncomfortable' situations that might arise? Christians will handle these situations differently, depending on how they understand Scripture, and the freedom of their conscience before the Lord when it comes to (what I will call) 'questionable' matters (1 Corinthians 8:1-13). If non-believers are taking God's name in vain, for example, some Christians will feel it is their duty to 'stand up for God's honour' by asking their guests not to do so in their home. No matter how briefly or sensitively we do this it will cause our guests to be embarrassed. Certainly long explanation about the issue, filled with Bible references, is not appropriate at this stage of the relationship. The worst thing to do to a guest is embarrass them. Nobody likes to be scolded or chastised and if we are chewed out we resent it. I have rebuked

Christians for taking the Lord's name in vain (because it grieves God) but I avoid reprimanding non-Christians because I have little or no expectation that non-Christians will conform to Christian moral standards. In time they realize that coarse language is inappropriate around you and in your home. For them it is a bad habit and they know they should not use foul language in certain contexts. When they occasionally lapse into these bad habits they usually offer an unsolicited apology.

Personally I would not intervene in such a situation unless my guest did it very often or in an especially vulgar manner. In that situation the guest will not be surprised at all to be asked to modify his behaviour because this is just common manners. God has not given us the responsibility of policing everything non-believers do. We can show them by our own 'clean' speech that we don't use God's name that way. Later, if the Lord allows the relationship to develop, perhaps we can talk about this and explain why, but for now, especially in the early stages of building a relationship, we should be willing to let it go.

If a non-believing guest asks if they can smoke (and I think most will ask, instead of just lighting up) we can allow it or politely say we would prefer if they did not. I have been in the opposite situation as a guest in the home of a non-Christian when they ask if it is okay to have a cigarette! But if it were my call in my home I would suggest (weather permitting) that if they must they should step out into the back garden so they can smoke there. This is perfectly acceptable in a culture that understands the health hazard of passive smoking. A Christian friend has a sign in his home that says 'If you smoke we will assume you are on fire and call the fire brigade!' People who see it usually get the message. We don't want to create artificial and unnecessary barriers in fledgling relationships. In trying to build friendships we should refrain from any uninvited lectures we might be tempted to give about the harmful effects of cigarettes or how the body is the Lord's temple, because (in the latter case) that is not true for a non-believer. Our guests should know that their smoking is not an insurmountable obstacle in our desire to build a relationship with them.

What should we do if our guest brings a bottle of wine as a courtesy? Some believers would be happy to drink it with them but some might not feel free in conscience to do this. If this is the case they could thank the guest for the thoughtfulness, graciously decline the offer, and return the bottle of wine to them, saying, 'We don't drink alcohol.' But I think it would be preferable to accept their gift and offer to serve them but not partake yourself. It is unlikely they will bring a bottle of wine again because it would be disrespectful of the host's sensibilities. Most people understand the cut and thrust of social interaction.

If we are going to spend time with non-believers and invite them into our homes and accept invitations from them to go to their homes we need to behave in a loving and sensitive manner, regardless of what our personal convictions are. We should not major on minor issues or make mountains out of molehills. It is not that smoking and drinking alcohol are unimportant or irrelevant but they are secondary issues and we should remember that. No right thinking individual will expect you to compromise your convictions for the sake of friendship with them.

With a little imagination we should capitalize on holidays and special occasions such as Christmas, New Year's Eve and New Year's Day, Labour Day, Memorial Day, Thanksgiving, Easter, Valentine's Day, Mother's Day, Father's Day, the Fourth of July, Halloween, St George's Day, St David's Day, St Andrew's Day and St Patrick's Day (I'm Irish). It is not necessary on such occasions to have a devotion or gospel presentation because the goal is simply to get acquainted with non-Christians at this stage in the process of evangelism. We need to be especially sensitive to widows, widowers, one-parent families, college students and others who are often alone during the holidays and on special occasions. Not only will we be building relationships with these people by inviting them to join us but we will also be ministering to them in a very real and tangible way that many of them will not soon forget.

We need to be available when non-believers are hurting and need help. Life can be tough. Many people are hurting, sad, bereaved, bored, lonely, frustrated, and anxious. People get ill, experience marital problems, worry about their children, and lose their jobs. These and other difficult situations give us an opportunity to express Christ's love. This is not about exploiting vulnerable people, rather it is about ministering to them. Ask yourself what you can do in the situation and then do it. Can you baby-sit or mow the lawn? There is a host of other ways to show that we care. And, let's not forget that part of building a relationship with non-believers includes letting them do some things for us. Rather than asking people in the church to keep an eye on your house while you are away, why not ask a neighbour to do it?

As the relationship develops we need to be careful about insisting our non-believing friends switch cultures — i.e. of giving them the impression they need to start trying to live like a Christian before they have made a profession of faith in Christ. Too often we Christians expect non-believers to change their behaviour before they have made a profession of faith in Christ.

Do our non-believing friends and acquaintances need to stop committing adultery or fornication? Yes! Do they need to stop getting drunk? Yes! In other words, do they need to stop sinning and start living a righteous life? Yes! Of course they do! But there is something they need to do first, before they can stop doing these things, and that is to repent of their sin and profess faith in Jesus Christ.

Suppose the problem is adultery, and our relationship with our non-believing friend has progressed to the point that he feels comfortable asking us what we think (an unlikely scenario because if a man is going to cheat on his wife he is probably not going to tell his mates about it). We should be unequivocal about what the Bible says and what God's holy standards are. We should tell them that adultery and every other form of immorality is sin (Exodus 20:14). But we shouldn't stop there. If our non-believing friend is still willing to listen, we need to go on and explain that Scripture says no one can obey God's commands on their own, especially those who are still dead in their sins and trespasses (Ephesians 2:1-3), and that they need to come to faith in Christ.

A gospel conversation

When we hear the word 'witness', we usually think of someone who tells others what they know. A witness is someone who 'proclaims' what they have 'seen and heard' (1 John 1:3). In other words, a witness is someone who speaks up about an important matter — who testifies verbally in a court of law — or has something valuable to say and says it. If we are going to be Christ's witnesses then we need to speak up. We need to tell those with whom we have been building a friendship what we know about Christ and God's plan of salvation. In other words, there must be a conscious effort to steer our conversations in this direction and to do so tactfully. Jesus came into Galilee, proclaiming the gospel of God, and saying, 'The time is fulfilled, and the kingdom of God is at hand; repent and believe in the gospel' (Mark 1:14-15). Ours is the same message as that of the Master.

What should we include in our conversations? The friendship method of evangelism is more of a give-and-take exchange — more of a back-and-forth discussion — as opposed to the one-sided 'I'll-do-the-talking-while-you-do-the-listening' kind of stereotypical presentation often associated with other witnessing methods. It will probably take several of these back-and-forth conversations before we are able to get everything across. We all need to be familiar with an abridged version (at least) of the gospel. This can be expanded as opportunity allows. First, we cannot assume that people today (in any culture) have an accurate or even a working knowledge of what the Scriptures really teach.

Where to begin?

If the church is to be dedicated to glorifying God and being obedient to the call of Christ then it needs to diligently seek the lost by sharing with them the good news of the gospel. The necessity to engage in witnessing for Christ should be preached from the pulpit.

Many condensed versions of the gospel encourage the presentation of the good news in a logical manner. Such A, B, C approaches are helpful to a certain degree but all human plans have their downside. The downside with many condensed versions of the gospel is that they tend to depend on the Christian being able to maintain control of the conversation. The problem is we can't always control the conversation in the way we would like, irrespective of the techniques we use.

Spiritual conversations with non-believers can be like trying to mind mice at a crossroads! Not every discussion starts at point 'A'. Some start at point 'C' or even worse, they start at point 'X' or 'Y'. At other times our spiritual conversations with non-believers meander from point 'A' to point 'F', back to point 'A' or 'B', then off to point 'X', despite our best efforts to stay on track. It is good to have a logical set of steps in our head to work from but we should not be so tied to the sequence that we don't know what to say whenever the conversation takes an unexpected turn.

Many condensed presentations of the gospel use the idea that 'God loves you' as their point of contact with non-Christians. The often neglected truth that 'God made you' can be a good starting place in our conversations. The underlying idea we need to expand on is that since God made us he has authority over our lives and our eternal destiny (Romans 9:20-21). Undoubtedly this can lead to complicated discussions which focus on creation apologetics and this can be a difficult battleground for the inexperienced warrior.

Where we begin our conversation will depend on the kinds of questions or comments that our non-believing friends have uttered. People need to understand (not perfectly, but at least in some basic way) that God is the sovereign ruler and creator of all things, including themselves (Genesis 1:27; Psalm 100:3; Job 42:2; Daniel 4:35). We live in a time when many people are interested in exploring spirituality, even if they are not particularly interested in the spiritual truths found in Scripture. Many people would describe themselves as 'not religious' but 'spiritual'.

The notion of the secularization of society has influenced Christian apologetic strategy. But perhaps we need to rethink our approach because although many people are hedonistic there are a great number of people interested in the spiritual dimension of life. Many of them are misguided and misinformed about the true nature of spirituality and so there is a growth in New Age spirituality, paganism, the cults, minority religions and fundamentalist and radical quasi-political-religious movements. The reality is that we live in a time when many people are fascinated by things like world religions, mysticism, occult or psychic phenomena without necessarily being attracted to the Scriptures. Thus we need to approach every conversation about spiritual matters with our non-believing friends from the premise that they have little or no true knowledge regarding the God of Scripture. Their ideas about God are essentially man-made, as opposed to being based on what the Bible actually says. Their 'god' is not the Great and Holy One of the Old and New Testaments, but the product of their own foolish hearts and spiritually darkened minds (Romans 1:21).

So when we talk with people about God, we need to speak of as many of his glorious attributes as possible and not just the one or two non-believers enjoy emphasizing (like his love and forgiveness), to the exclusion of others (like his justice and wrath) thereby getting a distorted or even an idolatrous idea of who God is. God has many attributes non-believers need to hear about, even if they end up rejecting our witness — attributes like his holiness, majesty, omnipotence, sovereignty, patience, goodness, mercy, grace, wrath, justice, omniscience and transcendence. We should, however, avoid using such theological language in our discussions. Such words might be a kind of helpful shorthand for insiders but they are unfamiliar to outsiders and the point is to communicate effectively, efficiently, intelligently and sensitively. It takes effort to jettison the jargon.

'Be my witnesses'

Recently I was interviewed live via telephone on Christian radio that has a largely non-Christian audience (about one of my books which had just been published). Just before going on air the interviewer said, 'Please try to avoid any religious jargon.' I felt a sense of panic as I wondered if I could talk about the book without using 'jargon'. I managed to do it but I had to speak slowly while my mind was racing to find alternative words to express the ideas in more understandable terms. It was a challenge.

I would encourage would-be witnesses (all believers) to rehearse sharing their 'testimony' (a jargon word that needs to be replaced with, perhaps, their 'story') with a Christian friend who will interrupt every time you use a religious word (like 'salvation'). The one exception to this is the use of the word 'sin'. I always refer to sin as 'sin' but it is not a hill I am prepared to die on. Others have said we should use the word 'wrongdoing' instead and I can see some merit in doing that.

We should not be afraid that a discussion of God's attributes will raise thorny questions, like: 'If God is in control of everything and if he is a good God, why does he allow bad things to happen?' We must be honest and humble because we don't always know why God does the things he does (Isaiah 40:28). Scripture says that his ways are higher than ours (Isaiah 55:8-9). We live in a fallen world, in which man's sin has negatively impacted the whole creation (Romans 8:20-22). But God is able (and does) bring good out of life's difficulties, especially for his redeemed people (Genesis 50:20; Romans 8:28). Sometimes the problem with the kinds of questions non-believers ask is that we haven't figured out the answers ourselves — in which case, the best thing to say is, 'I don't know; that puzzles me, too.' We should never give smug answers to people who may be really struggling to understand a real difficulty in their lives.

Other times, however, the problem is we have the same doubts about God many of our non-believing friends have. Our own understanding of who God is and what he is like is deficient. Sometimes we have doubts because we have not been taught properly or because up to now we have been unwilling to believe the truth about him ourselves. In such cases, an honest answer to a non-believer's thorny question might be: 'I've wondered about that myself', or, 'I haven't figured that one out yet, either. But, here's what I do know...', and then move to some aspect of who God is that we are more knowledgeable about, and have fewer problems believing. Wherever possible we need to be prepared to give biblical answers, regardless of what non-believers may initially think.

Perhaps the first step in being a witness for Jesus is to work on settling some of our own doubts. The Holy Spirit will help if we pray for illumination and intensify our study of God's Word. The Bible is the inspired, inerrant, living Word of God. We must have confidence in its inspiration, inerrancy, canonicity and authority. We must believe in its veracity, its dynamic power and efficacy. We must be guided and governed by the Word of God in all matters of faith and practice. The Bible not only lays out God's plan of salvation for sinful mankind (2 Timothy 3:15), it also reveals many things about God himself — such as his true nature.

In fact, Scripture indicates God has revealed various things about his nature through creation (Psalm 19:1; Romans 1:20), and through his Son, Jesus Christ (Hebrews 1:1-3). Hence, there are actually three witnesses (Deuteronomy 19:15) — Scripture, creation, and Jesus. Therefore, if God has gone to the trouble of giving us three such powerful witnesses regarding himself we should not rush through this divine revelation to get to repentance and faith in Jesus. It is crucial that we ultimately get to that but we must start where people are at, and that conversation may be very far from the cross.

Christians tend to give non-believers the impression God is only love. But many non-believers' concepts of love are distorted by sentimentalism and emotionalism. Hence God's love has to be carefully explained from Scripture both in terms of what it is (1 John 4:10) as well as what it is not (Acts 17:30-31).

Love is not God's only attribute. To counterbalance the mistaken notion many non-believers have about God, Christians need to present some of his other attributes. For example, God's holiness has tremendous implications for the gospel (Habakkuk 1:13). We should not avoid talking about God's wrath (though the word 'wrath' itself is probably best replaced with 'anger') just because we are afraid how people may react. Scripture does not say (or imply) that 'God loves the sinner but hates his sin'. On the contrary, it says that God hates all who commit sin (Psalm 5:5; Psalm 7:11-13; Psalm 11:5). The point is not to take our non-believing friends through a check-list of God's attributes. Some of his attributes may never come up in our conversations and, therefore, do not need to be discussed. As we converse with our non-believing friends and discover what they believe about God, we need to make sure they hear about who he really is, because an accurate understanding of God is essential to understanding the gospel of God. People need to know about God's holiness along with man's sin and depravity (Exodus 15:11; Habakkuk 1:13; Romans 1:28-32; Ephesians 2:1-3).

The word 'gospel' means 'good news' but in order for people to appreciate the 'good news', they need to know about the 'bad news'. It is the bad news that puts the good news into perspective. The bad news is what makes the good news good!

Practical advice

So what is the bad news? The bad news is that all people are born into this world as sinners. Among other things that means we come into this world without any natural affection for God. We do not have any desire or instinct to please or obey God. God is holy. This means that he is pure and perfect, without sin or defect. Everything he does is right, and good, and just. God does not overlook sin nor will he permit anything corrupted by sin into his presence. Because we are sinners by nature as well as practice we are far more offensive and loathsome and disgusting and repulsive to God than we can possibly imagine.

Scripture says only the man or woman who has clean hands and a pure heart can stand in God's holy presence (Psalm 24:3). That effectively eliminates everyone because Scripture also says that all have sinned and fallen short of the glory of God (Romans 3:23). Apart from faith in Jesus Christ our hands are not clean, and apart from repenting and believing the gospel our hearts are anything but pure.

So what can we do to get these truths across to our non-believing friends? How do we help them see the great gulf (Luke 16:26) that exists between an infinitely holy God and corrupt depraved sinners? Without the regenerating work of the Holy Spirit (John 3:3-8) these truths will remain concealed from them (Luke 9:45).

As we converse with our non-believing friends we can try and show them, for example, how God made man in the beginning (Genesis 1:1); how he made men and women in his own image and likeness (Genesis 1:26-27); how he made them upright (Ecclesiastes 7:29), which means they were not sinners by nature or practice; how he placed them in an environment described as 'very good' (Genesis 1:31), and (so far as we know) gave them just one simple command to obey (Genesis 2:16-17). We can continue by pointing out that the Fall of mankind described in Genesis chapter three was far more devastating than most people realize. Adam and Eve chose to reject God by sinning against his command (Genesis 3:1-6), which plunged all mankind into sin and death (Romans 5:12). Ever since the Fall, men and women have been rejecting God's various testimonies regarding himself — choosing, instead, to believe an assortment of lies, rather than the truth (Romans 1:21).

Hence, all men and women are idolaters — because they refuse to worship the true God as he has revealed himself to them through creation, Scripture and Jesus Christ. In their lost condition, all people are idolaters — because they invariably choose to worship other gods, like money, sex, work, material possessions, power and popularity. Many people who claim to worship God are actually worshipping a god of their own imagination — not the true God as he has revealed himself. Furthermore, deep down sinful men and women know many of these things are true (Romans 1:32).

The good news is that God has made provision whereby sinful, offensive people can be forgiven and changed — whereby people can be redeemed and made clean — whereby the threat of God's wrath can be removed and replaced by his saving grace. The glorious message of the gospel is that Christ Jesus came into the world to save sinners. He calls sinners to repentance and faith.

Salvation comes from God. The psalmist David once said, 'Salvation belongs to the LORD' (Psalm 3:8). Jonah also said, 'Salvation belongs to the LORD!' (Jonah 2:9). In the book of Revelation the apostle John said he heard, 'the loud voice of a great multitude in heaven, crying out, "Hallelujah! Salvation and glory and power belong to our God, for his judgments are true and just ..."' (Revelation 19:1).

We need to convey to non-believers what God's requirements for salvation are. God requires repentance and faith (Mark 1:15) and so we need to explain carefully and accurately what this means. Repentance needs to be carefully defined because it involves far more than simply feeling bad about what we have done or only feeling remorse after being caught. Specifically, it includes admitting we have sinned against God (Psalm 51:4) and confessing we are sinners in his sight (Luke 18:13). It also includes confessing specific sins committed against God.

But there is even more to repentance than that. True repentance (in the biblical sense) brings about changes in a person's life. It is not that we become sinless (1 John 1:8, 10) but that there is a growing desire to turn away from the sins God finds so repugnant, and pursue a path of obedience to his laws. Hence, Scripture exhorts those who claim to have professed faith in Christ to 'bear fruit in keeping with repentance' (Matthew 3:8). Elsewhere, repentance is defined in Scripture as ceasing to do evil and learning to do what is good (Isaiah 1:16-17; Isaiah 55:7; 2 Timothy 2:22).

Repentance is so crucial to salvation Jesus said, 'unless you repent, you will ... perish' (Luke 13:3, 5). Likewise, as he went about preaching the gospel, the apostle Paul said, God 'commands all people everywhere to repent' (Acts 17:30). But that is not the whole story of repentance. Repentance also involves a growing hatred of the sin that continues to linger within us and the desires we still have to do things that are contrary to God's commands. Paul confessed that he struggled with this himself (Romans 7:15-24). This passage shows how much he hated the sin that remained in his life and how much he longed for the day when he would be set free from it once and for all. Those who repent will have a similar hatred of the sin that still lurks within them.

The other basic requirement for salvation our non-believing friends need to know about is 'faith' or 'belief'. Many non-believers will have an understanding of faith that is more humanistic than biblical. So it is up to us to help them grasp what the Bible means when it talks about faith. Biblical faith is not some vague wish or ethereal desire. Biblical faith has an assurance and unshakable conviction which is not based on human wisdom or wishful thinking. Biblical faith is established on the solid foundation of Jesus Christ's life, death and resurrection. Hence, the Scripture says, 'For God so loved the world, that he gave his only Son, that whoever believes in him should not perish but have eternal life' (John 3:16). Jesus also said, 'For this is the will of my Father, that everyone who looks on the Son and believes in him should have eternal life, and I will raise him up on the last day' (John 6:40). The book of Romans says, '... if you confess with your mouth that Jesus is Lord and believe in your heart that God raised him from the dead, you will be saved. For with the heart one believes and is justified, and with the mouth one confesses and is saved. For the Scripture says, "Everyone who believes in him will not be put to shame"' (Romans 10:9-11).

Faith in Christ is not a blind faith without evidence or reason, for we have God's own testimony in Scripture, in history, and in creation. We have biblical prophecies given hundreds and even thousands of years beforehand regarding the coming Saviour. We have a record of some of the miracles Jesus performed, not the least of which is his resurrection from the dead. We also have the existence of the Christian church despite centuries of persecution, along with the testimony of millions of men and women whose lives have been changed by the gospel of Jesus Christ. These and other evidences make faith in Christ a reasonable act, rather than some blind leap into the dark unknown.

The primary mission of the church of Christ is to be dedicated to glorifying God. In order to do this it must faithfully proclaim the whole truth of Scripture, without fear or favour. Any definition of mission must include the cross-cultural mandate to reach un-reached peoples. The unfinished task of mission is to provide access to the gospel to every tribe and tongue. This must be central to our vision casting. The Church needs to understand that God's plan for history is all about his glory covering the earth as the waters cover the sea and that is accomplished by raising up worshippers to him from every tribe and tongue (Revelation 5:9). Let us gossip the gospel for God's glory.

Note

1. Morton Scott, *Down-to-Earth Discipling: Essential Principles to Guide Your Personal Ministry*, NAV Press, 2003, p.38.

Conclusion

Every sincere Christian will want to fulfil the sacred duty and tremendous privilege of sharing the gospel. It is liberating to know that we do not have to be bound to one method of evangelism. In advocating relational evangelism this work offers many practical guidelines for being faithful witnesses. Evangelism is a two-way conversation that requires sensitive and flexible interaction which avoids religious jargon.

I trust we have dispelled any wrong notions about what a Christian is inasmuch as it does not refer to one who is religious, practising works of righteousness, being born into a Christian family, attending church regularly, practising religious duties, or having made some kind of public display of adherence to Christ. Being a Christian rather refers to a person who becomes aware of his or her sins, has become dependent on the grace of God, has received by faith the salvation made possible through the person and work of Christ, and whose life undergoes radical transformation.

A Christian is one who realizes, through the illuminating work of the Holy Spirit, that he or she is unworthy in God's sight —

being sinful by practice and by nature. A Christian becomes a new creation and this salvation belongs to anyone who is willing to come in repentance and faith to Jesus.

Christians should not automatically disassociate from non-Christians when they are converted, although this may be necessary in order to establish a clean break and to discontinue certain sinful practices. Rather we ought to look at Jesus as our model. He interacted with sinners who were regarded as unclean. He did so in order to influence them, and not to be influenced by them. He also mixed with them intentionally at the cost of harsh criticism by the religious people. He befriended them genuinely for the purpose of winning them.

No one method of evangelism fits all people, but each believer is to find his or her preferred method. Whether it is preaching; confrontational evangelism or relational evangelism, the issue of integrity is important. Christians should socialize with non-Christians because Jesus gives us this example. We might be misunderstood but so was Jesus! Socializing with non-Christians increases opportunities to share the gospel. In seeking to lead people to salvation we must be clear that it is a salvation from the wrath of God against sin, and not just separation from God because unbelievers are already separated from God. Furthermore, salvation is not from annihilation, it is salvation from hell. We must be honest and courageous in confronting false and popular notions, including universalism and salvation by works.

We need to be clear about divine sovereignty and human responsibility in relation to salvation. Whereas believers are not held responsible for the eternal destiny of people, they are responsible for obeying the Lord's instruction to be his witnesses. God's sovereignty in salvation allows believers not to be overly concerned with making the gospel palatable so as not to offend people. We do not have to feel we have failed if our efforts in evangelism do not bring the desired results. Essentially our witnessing and evangelism is always to be done to the glory of God.

So, let us befriend non-Christians and avoid the kind of legalism that forbids or disdains associating with sinners. Remember that is what we are: sinners saved by grace. Let us endeavour with God's help to live consistent Christian lives. Let us develop the skills of good listening and cultivate common interests with unbelievers, without compromising the integrity of the gospel. Let us be willing, able and ready to share our conversion experience. People love personal stories! Let us invite non-believers to our homes but refrain from holding non-Christians to the same standards as Christians, especially with regard to smoking, drinking and the use of language. There are so many opportunities if we just give it a little thought.

Witnessing comes from a living and dynamic relationship with Christ and is established on true knowledge (experiential and biblical) of the gospel. If we are to be effective witnesses then we must ask God to enable us through the power of the Holy Spirit. We must never forget our utter dependence on the Holy Spirit. Every believer is called to wholehearted obedience in engaging as active witnesses for Christ. A consistent Christian life will naturally open doors to share the good news. To do this, believers must engage in fervent and frequent prayer for opportunities, look for the ones the Lord sends, and know what to do when these opportunities arise.

May the Lord be glorified in all our conversations, especially those that are about who God is and what he has done for us in Christ! *Soli Deo gloria!*